Colorful Angles

Triangles, Diamonds & Hexagons With a Contemporary Look

by Susan Stein

INTERNATIONAL

95 Mayhill Street
Saddle Brook, NJ

Acknowledgements

Photography: Michael Keefe, St. Paul, Minnesota.

Graphic Designers: Mimi and John Shimp of SPPS, Inc., Las Vegas, Nevada.

Fabric used on the cover is a hand dyed and silk screen from Lunn Fabrics.

Sources for the dyed fabrics used in the book are :

Cherrywood Quilts and Fabrics, 361 Cherrywood Drive N, Baxter, MN 56401, 218-829-0967. Send $5.00 for swatch card.

Lunn Fabrics, 357 Santa Fe Drive, Denver, CO 80223, 303-623-2710.

Shades, Inc.., 2880 Holcomb Bridge Road, Suite B-9, Alpharetta, GA 30202, 800-783-DYED.

Artspoken Yardage, Marit Lee Kucera, 30 S. St Albans Street , St. Paul, MN 55105, 612-222-2483. Send color sample of what you want. Silk and cotton available.

Second printing. Printed in Hong Kong.

ISBN: 1-881588-03-3

Table of Contents

The Basics

Fabric Selection & Figuring Yardage 5
General Piecing Instructions 5
Batting, Machine Quilting 6
Grid Quilting 6
Outline Quilting 6
Stencil Designs 7
Stipple Quilting...7
Binding..7
Borders 7
Use of Cutting Tools...7

Tool Instruction

Using Easy Angle™ & Easy Angle II™ 8
Using Companion Angle™ 9
Using Easy Eight™ 10
Setting In: The Eight Pointed Star...11
Using Easy Hexagon™ 12
Using SPEED GRIDS® 13
Trapezoids 14

Patterns

Majestic Star 15
String Star 19
Grid Star 23
Double X 25
Diamonds and Rust..27
Triangles Squared..29
Bears..31
Kokopeli 45
Tiger Lilies...52
Autumn...55
Sunflowers 57
Variable Star...61
Hayes Corner 63
Snail's Trail..65
Textured Pinwheels...67
Triangle Collage...70

Photographs 33-45

The Basics
&
Tool Tutorial

Fabric Selection and Figuring Yardage

Many projects in the book feature a strong print along with a dyed gradation or blend of colors. This results in a dramatic, textured, and contemporary look. Other fabrics may be selected for a country or decorator look or you may choose an "instant antique" look with small prints and shrinking after construction. The only way to gain confidence in the choosing of colors is to do it often, even if you just pile up bolts at the quilt shop to see what they look like.

Using dyed fabric bundles that are already coordinated is an easy way to guarantee a successful color scheme. The bundles usually consist of fat eighths – 9" by 19" pieces, fat quarters – 18" by 19" pieces or half yards – 18" by 38". Bundles contain six or eight fabrics. If using commercial yardage instead of hand dyed fabric, substitute $1/4$ yards for fat eighths and $1/3$ yards for fat quarters to allow for shrinkage and straightening. All fabrics used in the sample quilts are 100% cotton and the amounts given allow for some shrinkage. Borders are pieced if longer than one width of fabric unless cutting directions indicate cutting a strip from the lengthwise grain. Border seams are placed randomly and sewn at a 45° angle to hide them better.

Yardage is not given for backings because there are a variety of ways to do them. A popular trend is to piece a back that coordinates with the front of the quilt. Some people prefer to use 90" wide backing fabric instead of piecing at all. I often use two lengths of solid color fabric with a pieced panel of fabric from the quilt top down the center. Figure the width of most cotton fabric after shrinking at 40"- 42" and make the backing 2" larger than the quilt top.

General Piecing Instructions

All techniques used in this book are machine methods – piecing, appliqué, and quilting. For basic information, the Singer Sewing Reference Library book, *Quilting By Machine* is recommended. In addition, hints are included in individual lessons.

All seams are $1/4$" unless otherwise indicated. Seams begin at raw edges unless backstitching is specified and most sewing is done chain fashion with pairs of pieces fed under the needle one after the other without cutting the thread. Seam allowances are pressed to one side, usually toward the darker fabric. Points are trimmed from the corners of triangle squares. (See page 10.)

When pressing sets of strips, lay the strips back to front on the ironing board instead of side to side. This helps to prevent curving of the strips. In general, blocks are not pressed until bias edges have been sewn, but if it is necessary to press bias do so very carefully. Also, try to press so as to reduce bulk and avoid making thick spots shiny with too much heat and pressure. Press lightly from the back to guide seam allowances the way you want them to go and then press from the front to ensure that there are no "pleats" along seam lines.

Some instructions refer to the placing of pieces on the wall before sewing them into blocks. Use a fleece type of batting glued to the wall, a piece of covered insulation board, or a piece of felt, flannel, or fleece taped to the wall or pinned to the drapes to provide a surface that will hold cut triangles, squares, etc., without pinning so that they can be arranged easily. It is essential to be able to see a project vertically on the wall if you are using light to dark variations in color across the quilt top or a variety of elements in the design. It is much better to discard a few triangles than to make a quilt top that you are unhappy with in the end. Sometimes it is wise to let a project stay on the wall for a day or two so you can glance at it when doing other things and make changes. The wall is also helpful to "audition" border fabrics after the quilt blocks are sewn together.

Batting, Machine Quilting

For wallhangings, cotton/polyester batting is recommended as it is thin, but sturdy enough to allow pieces to hang flat on the wall. It needs to be quilted only every 4" or so. For bed quilts, cotton/polyester batting is fine, but polyester may provide more loft and warmth. If you do not want an "instant antique" or puckered look to your finished quilt, preshrink the cotton/polyester batts according to the directions included in the packages.

Machine quilting techniques used in the samples include:

Grid Quilting – Draw lines on open area extending from piecing, or fill in with overall crossing lines.

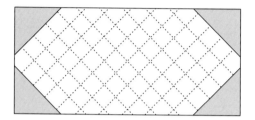

"Ditch" Quilting – or quilting in the seams – use a walking foot or even-feed foot to sew on the side of the seam where there are no seam allowances underneath.

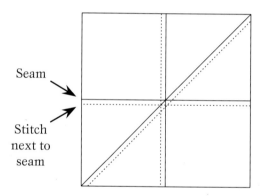

Outline Quilting – Use a darning foot to outline appliqué designs or a printed fabric motif.

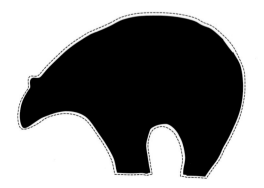

Stencil Designs – Use a purchased stencil for blocks and borders. Draw the design onto the quilt top, then quilt using a walking foot; or draw a design onto the quilt top and quilt with a darning foot and no feed dogs. You may also want to use the preprinted Stitch-Thru™ stencils from EZ International. Two of the designs are shown below.

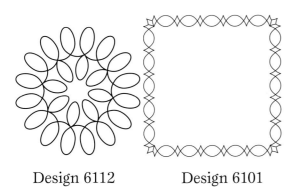

Design 6112   Design 6101

Stipple Quilting – Use darning foot to meander around an area in a random fashion to flatten it and create texture.

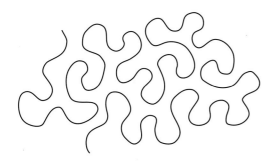

Binding – Most of the samples are bound with 2½" wide strips of fabric. Cut binding crosswise or lengthwise according to the fabric you have and connect the strips end to end with angled seams to reduce bulk. Fold in half with wrong sides together and sew to the edge of the quilt top through batting and back. Trim off excess batting and backing ¼" from edges of top and binding strip. Turn folded edge of binding around to the back of the quilt, pin it over the first stitching line, and sew in the seam line from the front, catching the edge of

the binding on the back. Each side of the quilt is bound separately, and the ends of the last two sides are folded in to make sharp corners.

Borders – Measurements to cut border strips are given, but it is best to cut these after the top is pieced. I recommend that you measure the quilt across the middle point in each direction, then cut (and piece strips, if necessary) this exact measurement. In some instances your quilt will be slightly larger (or smaller) at the edges, but taking this average measurement is the best way to have a flat quilt.

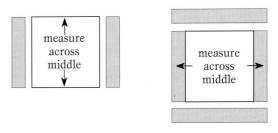

Use of Cutting Tools

The quilt designs in this book use EZ International cutting tools and a tutorial follows.

Additional tools needed are rotary cutter, mat, sewing machine, scissors, thread – the tools you use every day for your quilting projects.

Additional EZ International tools that may be used with projects in this book include:

- Quilter's Tool Handle
- Quickline Rulers
- Second Cut™ Ruler
- Appliqué Needles
- Stick n' Stitch
- Quilt Clips
- Stitch-Thru™
- Quilting Needles
- Giant Gridded Template Plastic

Using Easy Angle™ and Easy Angle II™

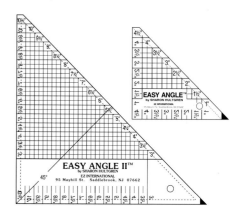

The Easy Angle™ and Easy Angle II™ make cutting triangles with equal sides a snap. As a bonus, it also makes fast and accurate squares from the same size strip as the triangles.

The Easy Angle™ is for triangles in the range of 1" to 4½" while the Easy Angle II™ has the range of 3" to 10½". Both tools are used the same way.

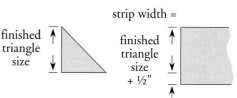

Step-by-Step Instructions:

Step 1: Determine your finished triangle size. Add ½" to get your unfinished triangle size.

Step 2: Cut the fabric strip the size of your unfinished triangle. For example, a 2" finished triangle would need a fabric strip of 2½".

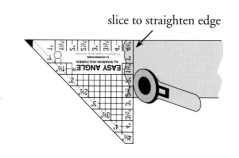

slice to straighten edge

Step 3: Lay fabric strip on the cutting mat in up to four layers, right sides together. Straighten the end of fabric strip by using the square corner of the tool and slicing.

Step 4: Turn tool so the words "Easy Angle™" read right side up and the black tip of the tool is at the right bottom corner.

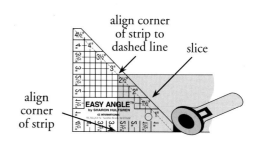

align corner of strip to dashed line   slice

align corner of strip

Step 5: Align the bottom of tool on the bottom edge of the fabric and slide until the dashed line is at the top left corner of fabric. (Your unfinished triangle size should also line up on the bottom and top left grid marks.) Slice along diagonal side.

Step 6: Take the square corner of tool and flip over so the corner is now at the top right. (The words "Easy Angle™" are now reversed, but the black tip of the tool remains at the bottom right side.)

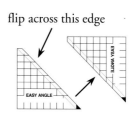

flip across this edge

Step 7: Align the left diagonal edge of the tool to the cut fabric edge and slide until the black tip hangs over the bottom fabric edge. (Your unfinished triangle size should also line up on the left and right top grid marks.) Slice along straight side.

Step 8: Continue steps 4 through 7 until you have made all your triangles.

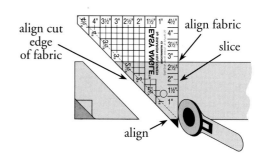

align cut edge of fabric   align fabric   slice   align

Using Companion Angle™

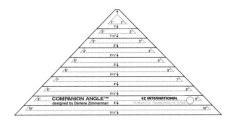

The Companion Angle™ is a quick and accurate way to make the long edge of a triangle with equal sides on the straight of the grain to prevent distortion on the outside of a block, border or quilt.

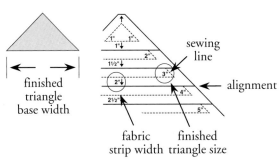

Step-by-Step Instructions:

Step 1: Determine the required size of the long edge of your finished triangle.

Step 2: Align the tool so that the words "Companion Angle™" can be read. The dashed lines represent sewing lines and show the finished triangle size, based on a ¼" seam allowance; center numbers represent the width of the strip to cut and solid lines underneath are used for alignment. (For example, cut a 2" strip for a finished 3" triangle.) Cut your fabric strip to the correct size using a ruler.

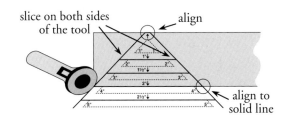

Step 3: Align tool with edge of strip. Carefully slice on both sides of the tool.

Step 4: Turn the tool so the words "Companion Angle™" are upside down.

Step 5: Align tool with edge of strip. Carefully slice on right side of the tool.

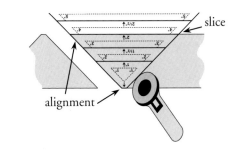

Step 6: Continue steps 3 through 5 until you have cut all your triangles.

Use Companion Angle™ with the Easy Angle™ or Easy Angle II™ to get perfectly compatible triangles. Simply use the same width strips and line up with equivalent alignments. For example, 2½" strips would require aligning fabric using the 2½" lines on both tools.

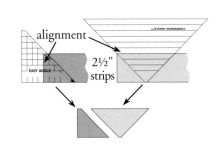

Use Companion Angle™ with the Easy Eight™ to get perfectly matching pieces. Use the same width strips and align the Companion Angle™ top with the strip edge.

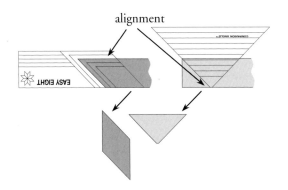

Using Easy Eight™

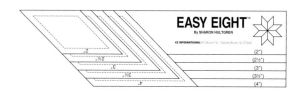

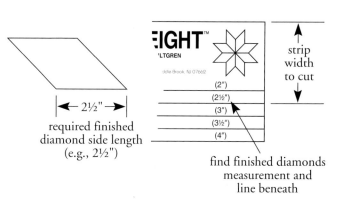

required finished diamond side length (e.g., 2½")

strip width to cut

find finished diamonds measurement and line beneath

The Easy Eight™ takes the difficulty out of making diamonds used in eight-pointed stars. It will make diamonds with seam allowances in sizes from 1" to 4" without templates or marking.

Step-by-Step Instructions:

Step 1: Determine the length of a side of your finished diamond.

Step 2: Use the numbers in parenthesis and the straight grid marks on the tool as a ruler to cut your fabric strip, but do not use a standard ruler because the tool grid will automatically convert the finished diamond to the correct fabric strip size. Fold fabric if necessary and cut.

Step 3: Turn the tool so the diamond grids are on the right and the numbers are readable.

Step 4: Trim the excess triangle off the left side of strip by aligning the bottom fabric edge and sliding until the top corner of the fabric is lined with the tool. Slice.

Step 5: Slide the tool to the right until the solid black diamond grid fits all around the top and cut edge of the fabric strip. Slice.

Step 6: Continue repeating step 5 until you have cut all your diamonds.

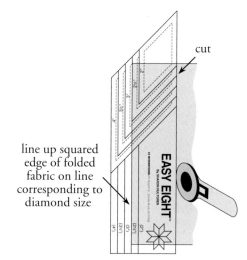

cut

line up squared edge of folded fabric on line corresponding to diamond size

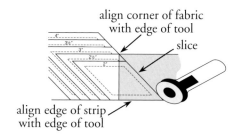

align corner of fabric with edge of tool

slice

align edge of strip with edge of tool

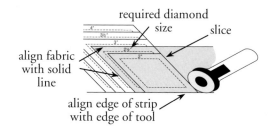

required diamond size

slice

align fabric with solid line

align edge of strip with edge of tool

Setting In: The Eight Pointed Star

These steps will be used several times in the construction of the Eight Pointed Star. They apply to setting in either a triangle or a square between two diamonds. The diamonds may be completely separate or may be part of another piece. The illustrations below assume piecing a triangle.

First align the triangle point with the point of the diamond right sides together, and stitch. Sew up to ¼" of the adjacent corner of the point and backstitch (for strength.)

Open and press in the direction of the arrow. You will press all of these in the direction indicated in the figure.

Lay this sewn piece right sides together over the second diamond and align as before. Backstitch at the beginning and stitch from the seam allowance at the center to the points.

Press down as before.

Gently fold the piece in half, right sides together, as indicated in the figure. Align the two points of the diamonds. Starting at your previous stitching; stitch to the points.

Open up and press the seam open or to one side. Trim the "dog-ears".

This technique may be used to set in the triangles and squares as shown on the next pages. Use it any time two diamonds come together with a set in square or triangle – and you are using the EZ Tools.

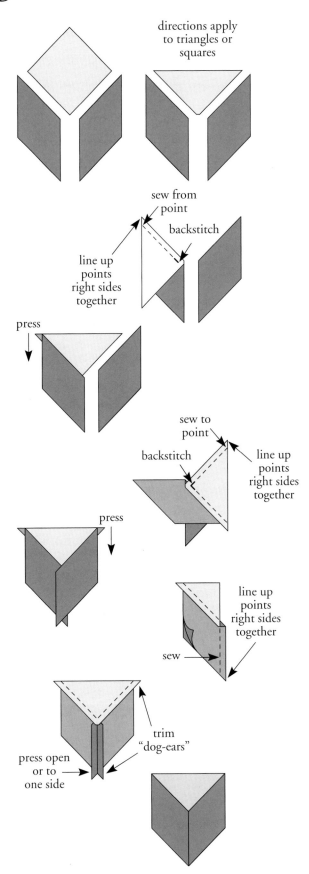

11

Using Easy Hexagon™

The Easy Hexagon™ is designed so that you can cut the strip and the hexagon shape with a rotary cutter. The hexagons are given in five different sizes and the length of the finished edge is given. Fabric should be folded once with the selvege edges together and then folded again bringing the fold to the selveges. Now select the size hexagon you want to use.

Set the straightened bottom edge of the fabric on the bold line that indicates the size you have chosen. Cut along the top edge of the Easy Hexagon™.

Rotate the Easy Hexagon™ so that the hexagon shapes are on the right hand side of this tool.

Line the bottom edge of the fabric strip on the bottom edge of the Easy Hexagon™. Note that the bold 2" line is now on the top edge of the fabric.

Open the fabric strip so the fabric is only folded once. Place the selvege edge on the left. Slide the Easy Hexagon™ to the left.

Cut along the Easy Hexagon™ as shown.

Turn diamond shapes.

Set diamond shape under the Easy Hexagon™ and trim the small triangles.

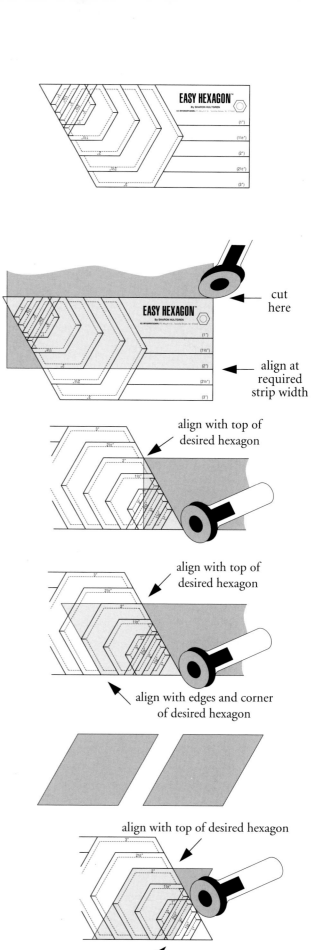

cut here

align at required strip width

align with top of desired hexagon

align with top of desired hexagon

align with edges and corner of desired hexagon

align with top of desired hexagon

align with edges and corner of desired hexagon

12

Set diamond shape under the Easy Hexagon™ and trim the small triangles on the other side.

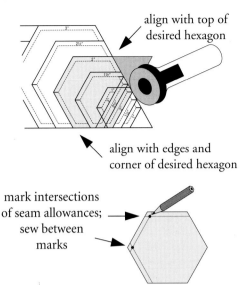

align with top of desired hexagon

align with edges and corner of desired hexagon

Hexagons are now ready for piecing.

mark intersections of seam allowances; sew between marks

Using SPEED GRIDS®

Quick-pieced triangles can be simplified by using the SPEED GRIDS®. They are available in ½", 1", 2", and 3" finished sizes.

Step-by-Step Instructions:

Step 1: Use the grid to trace the lines on the wrong side of your first fabric.

Step 2: Place the two fabrics right sides together and sew along the dashed diagonal lines.

Step 3: Using a ruler and a rotary cutter, cut on the solid lines and between the dashed lines.

Step 4: Pick apart sewn corners and open at sewn line to form a quick-pieced triangle.

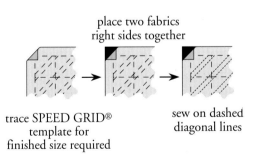

place two fabrics right sides together

trace SPEED GRID® template for finished size required

sew on dashed diagonal lines

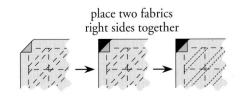

place two fabrics right sides together

Trapezoids

To cut any trapezoid with Companion Angle™, you need to measure the finished width of the base and the finished height. Add ½" to the height (two ¼" seam allowances to get the strip width.)

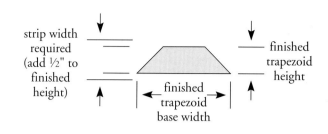

On the tool, find the dashed line for the desired finished base width. The solid line directly beneath will be the line on which to align your fabric.

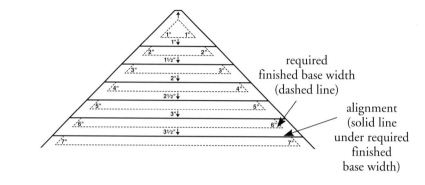

Align the fabric strip to the line so it extends on both sides of the tool. Cut on both sides of the tool.

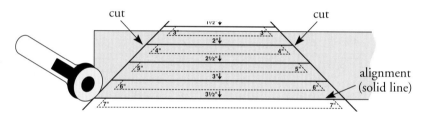

Invert the tool and align the top of the strip with the solid line and the cut edge of the fabric. Cut on the right.

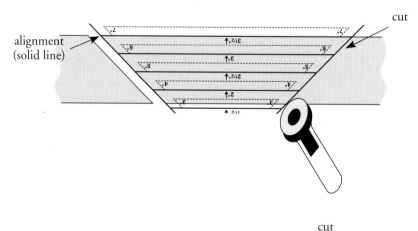

The alignment line on Companion Angle™ for trapezoids will be the line under the line representing the required finished base width. If the finished width is a whole number of inches (e.g., 6"), use the solid line underneath the appropriate dashed line. If it includes a half-inch (e.g., 5½") use the next higher (e.g., 6") dashed line for alignment.

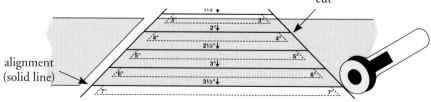

14

Quilt Designs & Instructions

Majestic Star
48" square
See Photograph page 37.

This wallhanging or lap robe began with a drapery sample that contains several shades of purple and rust. Solid colors were chosen for piecing to highlight the print of the drapery fabric and to allow subtle differences in color between identical shapes in the blocks, adding interest to the simple patterns. It is essential to cut out pieces and view them on the wall before sewing so that choices can be made and changed easily for maximum impact. The addition of a print border adds texture without competing with the focal fabric.

Materials Needed:

- ³/₈ yard of each of 4 different Purples
- ¹/₄ yard each of 2 different Rusts
- ¹/₄ yard Lavender
- ¹/₃ yard Rose
- ⁵/₈ yard Black
- ³/₈ yard 48" wide drapery fabric OR
- ³/₄ yard regular cotton fabric
- ⁵/₈ yard for Border
- ¹/₂ yard for Binding

15

Cutting Directions:

Purple: Cut 3" wide strips across the width of three of the purple fabrics. Use Easy Angle™ (refer page 8) to cut forty triangles for the points of the small stars.

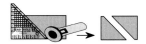

Cut four $5\frac{7}{8}$" squares of one of the purple fabrics in half diagonally to make eight triangles for points of middle sized star.

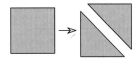

Cut two $11\frac{1}{4}$" squares from a medium purple and slice diagonally into four pieces to make eight triangles for outer edge next to the border.

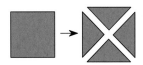

Rusts: Cut two strips of each rust fabric 3" wide. Use Easy Angle™ (refer to page 8) to cut 40 triangles and 20 squares.

Lavender: Cut a 3" wide strip into 16 triangles using Easy Angle™.

Rose: Cut a 3" wide strip into 16 triangles using Easy Angle™. Cut two $6\frac{1}{4}$" squares diagonally into four pieces to make 8 triangles. (See graphic above.)

Black: Cut one $7\frac{1}{2}$" wide strip into four $7\frac{1}{2}$" squares and one $5\frac{1}{2}$" square. Cut one 4" wide strip into squares and one $4\frac{1}{2}$" wide strip into four $4\frac{1}{2}$" squares (for border) and enough 4" squares to make a total of 12.

Drapery: Cut four $10\frac{7}{8}$" squares diagonally to make 8 triangles.

Border: Cut 4 strips $4\frac{1}{2}$" wide by the measurement through the middle of the quilt top after piecing and pressing. See page 7 for measuring the top. It will be approximately $40\frac{1}{2}$.

Binding: Cut 5 strips $2\frac{1}{2}$" wide.

Piecing Directions:

Before beginning to sew, place all pieces on a design wall to check for balance and effect.

Small stars for corners (make four):

1. Make 32 triangle squares using a variety of purple and rust fabric. You may want to use the Easy Angle™ tool for these triangles. Press, then trim off points.

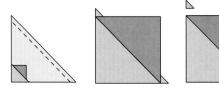

2. Sew lavender triangles to four 4" black squares by laying a square over long edge of a triangle, having points of triangle extending equally beyond corners of the square. Sew seam, repeat for opposite side of square. Press gently with seams toward triangles. Sew triangles to two remaining sides of square. Press.

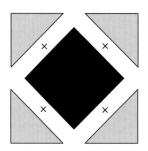

3. Form the rows by following the piecing diagram shown here:

Middle row

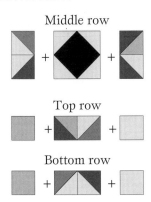

Top row

Bottom row

Sew these rows together to form the blocks, guiding seam allowances away from each other for better fit and less bulk. Press blocks.

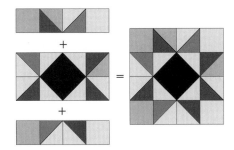

Small center star:

1. Repeat directions for small corner stars, substituting 5½" black square for center pieced unit.

Middle sized star:

1. Piece smaller rose triangles to four 4" black squares, following Step 2 of Small Stars.

2. Sew larger rose triangles to two adjacent edges of four more black squares, aligning square corners and guiding seam allowances toward triangles, forming large pieced triangles.

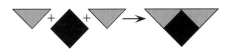

3. Sew two large purple triangles to each short side of the pieced triangles completed in Step 2. Add these units to opposite sides of small center star.

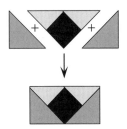

4. Complete top and bottom rows pieced triangles, purple triangles, and corner units. Add to block, press.

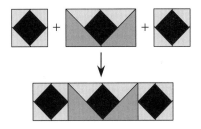

Large star:

1. Piece large drapery triangles to purple triangles and black squares as in middle sized star. Press seams away from drapery fabric as much as possible to reduce bulk.

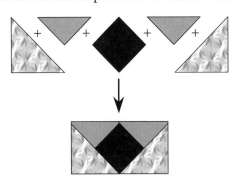

2. Assemble large star as in middle sized star. Press.

Piecing the Quilt Top:

After completing all the blocks, piece the top and borders following the diagram on the next page.

Sew the blocks together in rows, then sew the rows together. Piece and add borders.

Border:

1. Sew two border strips to opposite sides of quilt top, matching center of border with center of quilt top.

2. Add 4½" black squares to ends of two remaining border strips and sew borders to top and bottom edges of quilt top, matching centers and corners of squares to ends of the first two borders.

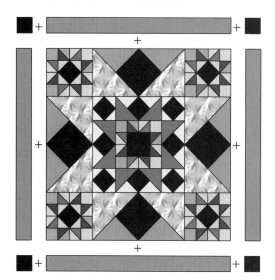

Finishing:

Baste layers. Quilt and Bind with 2½" wide strips.

Quilting methods include channel, free motion using a traditional motif, ditch, and outline.

I quilted straight lines in my borders, and lines radiating out from the large black diamonds in the side blocks and diagonal lines in the drapery fabric. In the large center star I quilted a quarter inch in from the seam line.

There are many ways to quilt this design, and feel free to be creative in your quilting. You may want to try one of the new Stitch-Thru™ designs such as one of the border motifs.

String Star

44" x 61" and 60" x 77"
See photograph page 35.

Smaller quilt shown here is 2 blocks x 3 blocks. Finished size is 44" x 61".

This star wallhanging needs only a bundle of dyed fabric in a light to dark gradation and a print fabric that contains several values of a single color plus an accent color. It is an old pattern that once used up lots of thin scraps left from other projects, which were pieced onto paper diamonds using the sew and flip method. Now we can create a wonderful contemporary look using color tricks and strip piecing methods in combination with the Easy Eight tool and rotary cutter.

Materials Needed:

Small Quilt:

- One bundle of six dyed fat quarters
- 1¼ yards Print fabric
- 1¼ yards Accent fabric for lattice, borders, and blocks
- ⅜ yard for Binding (2" strips)

Larger Quilt:

- One bundle of six dyed half yards
- 1⅞ yards Print fabric
- 2¼ yards Accent fabric for lattice, borders, and blocks
- ½ yard for Binding(2" strips)

Cutting Directions Small Quilt:

1. Cut fat quarters into 1¾" wide strips.

2. Cut three 4⅞" wide strips of accent fabric into squares and slice diagonally into 48 triangles.

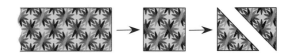

3. Cut two 4⅞" wide strips of print fabric into squares and slice diagonally into 24 triangles. (See above.)

4. Cut one 3½" wide strip of accent fabric into 12 squares for lattice.

5. Cut two 14" wide strips across width of print fabric. Slice into seventeen 3½" x 14" lattice strips.

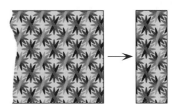

19

Cutting Directions Larger Quilt:

1. Cut half yards of dyed fabric into $1^3/_4$" wide strips.

2. Cut six $4^7/_8$" wide strips of accent fabric into squares and slice diagonally into 96 triangles. (See Step 2 for small quilt.)

3. Cut four $4^7/_8$" wide strips of print fabric into squares and slice diagonally into 48 triangles. (See Step 2 for small quilt.)

4. Cut two $3^1/_2$" wide strips of accent fabric into 20 squares for lattice.

5. Cut three 14" wide strips across print fabric. Slice into thirty-one $3^1/_2$" x 14" lattice strips. (See Step 5 for small quilt.)

Piecing:

1. Sew one dyed fabric strip of each color side by side, arranging them in order from light to dark. Make ten of these strip sets. Press seams of five sets toward dark side and seams of five sets toward light side.

2. Place one set of the light arrangement and one set of the dark arrangement right sides together, butting seams. Place Easy Eight™ on the strip sets with side angle points of the diamond on the center seam of the strip set, and the angled end of ruler at the left side of the strip set. Cut off ends of strips to start diamond as shown below. **Note**: Cutting tool will extend beyond edge of fabric – this will not affect piecing.

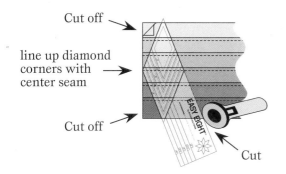

Cut off

line up diamond corners with center seam

Cut off

Cut

Turn Easy Eight™ around so you can complete cutting the right hand side of the diamonds, making sure side angle points are on the center seam line of the strip set.

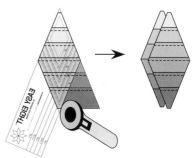

Cut four more pairs of diamonds from this strip set following the diagram below.

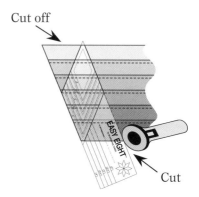

Cut off

Cut

Following Step 2, repeat the cutting sequence for the pairs of diamonds for the remaining strip sets.

3. Place two diamonds right sides together, with seams butting against each other. Starting on light colored end, sew from sharp point at raw edge to side angle of diamond, backstitching at center seam line. Make four pairs.

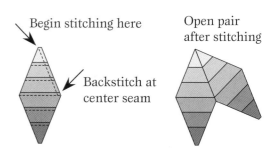

Begin stitching here

Backstitch at center seam

Open pair after stitching

Sew two pairs together, repeat, then sew two four diamond units together across entire middle seam, matching center points carefully. Whenever joining diamonds or halves of stars, seam allowances should be going in opposite directions to reduce bulk. Pin if necessary but try to use the seam allowances for matching as much as possible. Do not trim off points until the block is complete so that they can be used for matching.

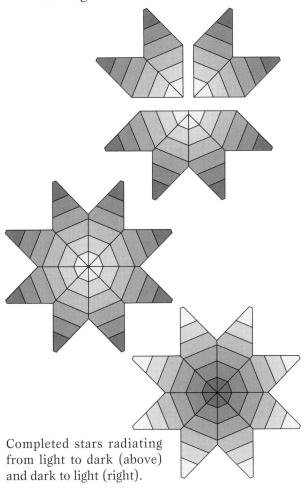

Completed stars radiating from light to dark (above) and dark to light (right).

4. Following the directions for Setting In: the Eight Pointed Star on page 11, sew accent triangles into spaces between points of the star, matching points with points of diamonds and sewing from raw edges into corners of star, backstitching 1/4" from inner corners. This is easier if you sew the first side of the triangle with the diamond on top so you can see end of previous stitching line. Sew second seam with triangle on top. Make three stars with light values in center and three stars with dark values in center. Press seam allowances away from diamonds, taking care not to stretch bias edges of triangles or center of star.

5. Add four print triangles to corners of star blocks, matching points. Trim off points. Press.

6. Arrange blocks into three rows of two blocks each (for small quilt) placing lattice strip on either side and between blocks, alternating light and dark centers. For larger quilt, arrange into four rows of three blocks each.

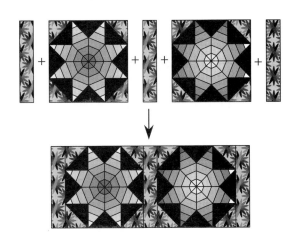

7. Connect two lattice strips end to end with squares of accent fabric (shown below) for small quilt. For larger quilt, connect three lattice strips with squares. Make four lattice/square sets for small quilt and five lattice/square sets for large quilt

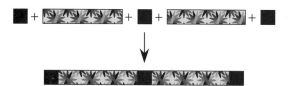

Piecing the Quilt Top:

After completing the rows of blocks and rows of lattice strips, you are ready to sew the rows together. Follow the diagram.

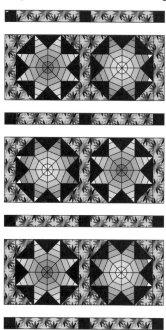

Borders

Measure quilt top across the middle after piecing. See page 7 for measuring and cutting directions. Add borders to top and bottom, then sides. For larger size quilt, you may need to piece border strips.

Baste layers. Quilt, and bind with 2" wide (cut) strips.

Larger quilt shown here is 3 blocks x 4 blocks. Finished size is 60" x 77".

Grid Star
42" square
See Photograph page 39.

This wallhanging features a great background print with subtle silver accents and lots of rose colored solids. The pattern appears to be the traditional eight-point star but is actually constructed as squares surrounded by parallelograms and triangles, which when assembled into rows create the stars at the intersections. Quilting extending from the seam lines creates a grid design in the plain squares and crosses the borders.

To make a queen size coverlet, multiply number of blocks by four and add borders to make desired size.

Materials Needed:

- scraps of solid color fabrics in light, medium, and dark values
- 3/4 yard print fabric (Tip: use a print that will look good when turned in different directions in the triangles.)
- 1/2 yard for Border
- 3/8 yard for Binding

Cutting Directions:

1. Cut 3" wide strips from scraps of solid colors. Cut off ends of strips with Easy Eight™ tool to begin 45° angle. Follow the directions for cutting diamonds on page 10. Cut strips into 3½" diamonds (72 total).

2. Cut print fabric into nine 7½" squares and two 4" wide strips. Slice 4" strips into thirty-six triangles using Easy Angle™.

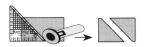

3. Cut four 3½" wide strips of border fabric and four 2½" wide strips of binding fabric.

Piecing Directions:

1. Place one lighter colored diamond right sides together with one print triangle. Triangles are sewn to bias edges of diamonds. Raw edges will match ¼" from sides, not at the points. Observe size of points extending beyond edges of each piece. Use this as a guide for piecing remaining seams. Stitch from raw edge to raw edge. Continue to feed pairs of diamonds and triangles under the needle until the 34 remaining lighter colored diamonds and background triangles are pieced.

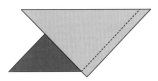

Place diamond and triangle right sides together.

2. Place darker colored diamonds right sides together with remaining sides of triangles, stitch from raw edge to raw edge, guiding first seam allowance away from triangle. Finger press seam away from triangle. After two diamonds are pieced to the triangle the long edges should be straight.

Grainline

3. Fold a large square in half both ways, making a finger crease at halfway point on all edges. Pin center of one side of square to center of a triangle-diamond unit. With square on top, backstitch to ¼" from corner, stitch across side making sure point of triangle is at seam line, and backstitch ¼" from raw edge at end of seam.

Dotted lines
represent fold lines

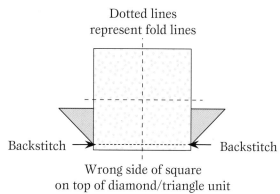

Backstitch ➡   ⬅ Backstitch

Wrong side of square
on top of diamond/triangle unit

Repeat this step for each side of the square. Place adjacent diamonds right sides together and stitch from outer raw edge to stitch line at corner of square, then backstitch. Press seams toward center square, making sure all seams are pressed without hidden pleats. Be careful not to stretch bias edges of triangles. Make nine blocks. Piece quilt top as a 9-patch – 3 blocks x 3 blocks.

Borders:

The border on this quilt has mitered corners, so the finishing is a little different. After measuring the top (see page 7) and cutting the border strips 6" longer, fold strips in half to find the center point. Also mark the place on the strip 3" before the ends. Match the center point of the strips with the center points of each side of the quilt. The place on the strips BEFORE THE 3" EXTENSIONS should match with the edges of the quilt top. Stitch borders to quilt beginning and ending ¼" from each edge. Place ends of border strips right sides together and stitch from the outside corner diagonally to the seam line.

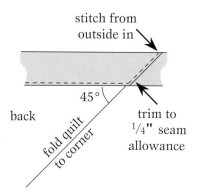

stitch from
outside in

45°

back   trim to
¼" seam
allowance

fold quilt to corner

Quilting in the sample is done with silver metallic thread to echo the silver in the print. All diagonal seam lines in the blocks are extended through the plain squares and borders. The seam lines between the blocks are also quilted in the ditch. Bind with 2½" strips.

Double X

28" square
See Photograph page 33.

Only 2½" of each solid color are required for this piece so it is a great way to use up the last of your dyed fabrics bundles. Pick a color washed background for a subtle color scheme or a black or navy solid for a dramatic look. This is a quick and easy wallhanging to make for an office or den.

Materials Needed:

- 4 values each from four different dyed fabric bundles (2½" strip of each)
- 1 yard Background (includes binding)

Cutting Directions:

1. Cut seven 2½" wide strips of background. Slice into 96 triangles and 48 squares using Easy Angle™.

2. From 2½" wide strips of sixteen dyed fabrics, cut 6 triangles of each. Leftover strips will go into borders.

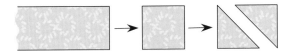

Piecing Directions:

1. Sew solid color triangles right sides together with background triangles to make triangle squares. (This step may also be done using Easy Angle™ if you cut the background strips the same length as the solid strips. Place right sides together and cut. (See page 8.) Press.

2. Assemble blocks using six triangle squares of one color and three background squares, pressing seam allowances in middle row toward center square. Press seams between rows toward center.

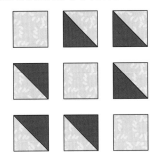

3. Arrange four blocks of different values of one color into large block, having lightest value diagonally across from darkest value. Make four large blocks.

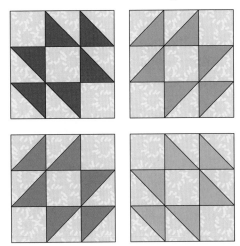

4. Sew these four large blocks together with lightest values in the center.

5. From scraps of colors, piece three strips each into four borders, trim to measurement of blocks. Cut four 2½" squares and add to ends of two borders. Sew shorter borders to top and bottom, borders with end squares to sides.

Top and bottom border

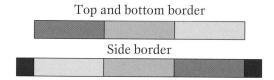

Side border

6. Layer, quilt, and bind with 2" cut strips.

Graphic below is enlarged to show the full quilt layout and the addition of the borders.

26

Diamonds and Rust

40" square
See Photograph page 42.

square diagonally to produce two triangles of each color. Layer next value of green with next value of gray and cut two squares, slice diagonally to produce 8 triangles. The third value will require three squares to produce 12 triangles, the fourth value will require 4 squares to produce 16 triangles, the fifth value 3 squares to make 12 triangles, the sixth value 2 squares to make 8 triangles, and the seventh value (darkest) will require 1 square to make 4 triangles.

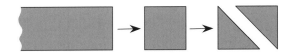

The use of four different color gradations makes it possible to play with the illusion of transparency and an inner light source, resulting in a dramatic wallhanging. If using bundles of dyed fat quarters, you will be able to use partial packs as long as you have enough to cut the pieces for the middle values. It is essential to cut all the pieces and view them from a distance as the color relationships can be very surprising. Replacing a color at this point is less expensive in time and money than having an unsuccessful finished quilt.

Materials Needed:

- one bundle of fat quarters or quarter yards of 7 gradations each of purples, grays, greens, and rusts (I usually leave off the lightest tint from the bundle of 8 fat quarters.)

Cutting Directions:

1. Layer lightest green with lightest gray and cut one $5^7/_8$" square. Cut through

2. Cut 3" wide strips of purples and cut triangles using Easy Angle™ (see page 8), according to numbers below:

lightest purple – #1 value, 8 triangles, #2 value, 16 triangles, #3 value, 24 triangles, #4 value, 32 triangles, #5 value, 24 triangles, #6 value, 16 triangles, #7 value (darkest) 8 triangles

3. Cut 3" strips of rusts and cut squares, according to numbers below:

#1 (lightest value) 4 squares, #2 value, 8 squares, #3 value, 12 squares, #4 value, 16 squares, #5 value, 12 squares, #6 value, 8 squares, and #7 value, (darkest) 4 squares

Piecing Directions:

1. Arrange all pieces on a piece of flannel or fleece hung on the wall. Dark greens,

grays, and rusts are on the outside edges and dark purples are in the center, as in the piecing diagram. (Also refer to the photograph on page 42.) Pin the pieces to the flannel or fleece and then remove it from the wall and place it on the floor next to your sewing machine. For sewing, remove one unit at a time.

2. Sew two purple triangles to adjacent sides of the rust squares, matching square corners, making larger triangles. Finger press seams toward triangles.

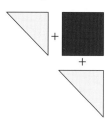

Place unit right sides together with gray or green triangle and sew long edges together to complete square units. Press seams toward plain triangles.

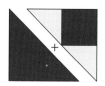

3. Sew pieced squares (64 total) into rows, making sure units are in proper order, and connect rows. Refer to piecing diagram below to keep you on track!

4. Baste layers, quilt, and bind with 2½" wide cut strips.

Piecing Diagram:

G = Green & Gray
R = Rust
P = Purple

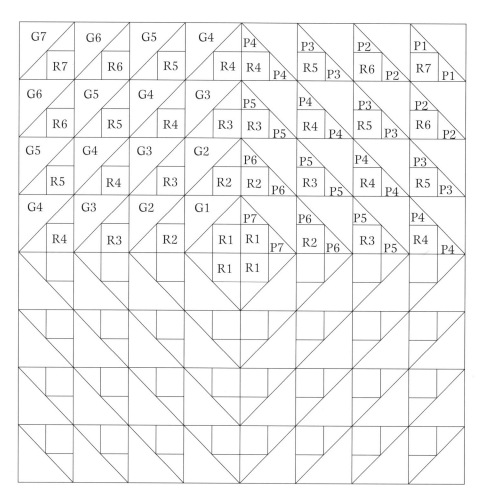

28

Triangles Squared
54" x 66"
See Photograph page 36.

This is a piece where you can play with all the different color values that come in bundles of dyed fabric. A design wall is essential to arranging the lights, mediums and darks, across the quilt surface. The stars provide the organization for the design but the background draws the eye around the whole quilt top to add motion and interest.

Materials Needed:

- 2 bundles (8 values each) of dyed fat quarters (sample uses brown and green plus a little gray)
- 1 yard Print fabric for Centers of stars
- ½ yard for Inner borders
- ⅞ yard for Borders
- ⅔ yard for Binding

Cutting Directions:

1. Cut twenty 6¼" squares from print fabric.

2. From star point fabrics, cut strips 3⅜" wide. Cut into triangles using Easy Angle™ (see page 8), eight triangles per star, 20 stars total.

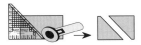

3. From background fabrics, cut strips 3⅜" wide; cut 4 squares and 8 triangles (using Easy Angle™) for each block.

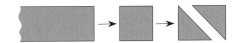

4. Cut eight 1½" wide strips of inner border fabric.

5. Cut eight 3½" strips of border fabric.

6. Cut seven 2½" wide strips of binding fabric.

Piecing Directions:

1. Sew star point triangles to background triangles, using mostly light colored background pieces with light colored star points but mixing in some medium and dark for interest. Mix medium values together with some light and dark added. Finally make triangle squares with mostly dark values. (Here is where you can play with pieces on the wall before sewing.) Press seams allowances toward darker color. Trim off points.

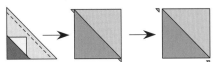

2. Follow these steps and refer to the graphics below for piecing one star. This quilt requires 20 stars.

Sew two triangle squares together and add to top of a print square. Repeat for bottom. Piece together two background squares and two triangle squares to make units for sides of block. Piece 20 blocks, gradually adding darker values as the blocks approach the bottom right hand corner of the quilt.

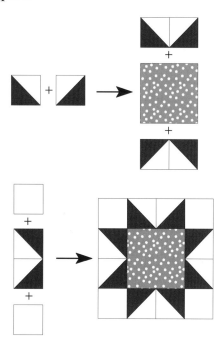

3. Arrange blocks on a design wall to check that the quilt top is interesting and colors aren't too "organized". Assemble blocks into rows. Sew rows together. See diagram to the right.

4. The border on this quilt has mitered corners, so the finishing is a little different. After measuring the top (see page 7) and cutting and piecing the border strips 6" longer, fold strips in half to find the center point. Also mark the 3" extension of each end. Match the center point of the strips with the center points of each side of the quilt. The ends of the strips BEFORE THE 3" EXTENSION should match with the

edges of the quilt top. Stitch borders to quilt beginning and ending ¼" from each edge. Place ends of border strips right sides together and stitch from the outside corner diagonally to the seam line.

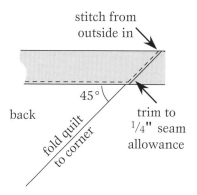

5. Quilting in the sample follows diagonals, crossing over background squares and print star centers. The border quilting was marked with three triangles cut from cardboard, placed randomly on inner and outer borders. Stitch-Thru™ stencils would also be appropriate for the open blocks and border.

30

Bears

35" x 47"

See Photograph page 42.

See Photograph page 42.

Materials Needed:

- 1⅛ yards Print fabric (scraps may be used with Easy Angle method)
- 1½ yards solid for Blocks and Borders
- ⅝ yard for Inner borders and Binding
- fabric for appliqués

Cutting Directions:

1. Cut print and solid fabric rectangles for 2½" SPEED GRIDS®. Make 184 triangle squares.

2. Cut twelve 4½" squares of the remaining fabric.

Cut for borders:

1. Cut four 3" wide strips of solid for borders.

2. Cut four 1" wide strips of inner border fabric. Of same fabric cut four or five 2 ½" wide strips for binding.

This *Ocean Wave* variation wallhanging is also the right size for a baby quilt and can be adapted to bed quilt size by making four times as many blocks. The appliqués can range from children's motifs to ducks for a sportsman. Or leave the quilt plain for a traditional look. The possibilities are endless and the pattern is a very simple one so let your imagination roam. SPEED GRIDS® – where the triangles are sewn in a large piece and then cut apart as triangle squares is used in this quilt.

Piecing Directions :

Piece using SPEED GRIDS® method:

1. Following directions on page 10, mark sew, and cut print and solid fabrics to make 184 triangle squares.

2. Sew four triangle squares together as in diagram. Make a total of 46 blocks. Press.

3. Sew blocks together with plain squares to make rows as shown in diagram. Sew rows together, guiding seams away from each other to reduce bulk and help match corners.

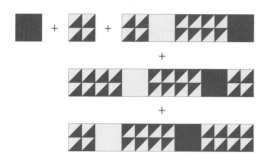

4. Sew inner borders to sides first to avoid having to piece them. Add inner borders to top and bottom.

5. Sew borders to sides first if you wish to avoid piecing them. In sample mitered borders were used; this will require more fabric. Add borders to top and bottom.

Applique:

1. (An excellent reference for machine appliqué is *Mastering Machine Appliqué*, by Harriet Hargrave.) Bear patterns are included on the pattern insert. Draw around design on front of appliqué fabric with chalk pencil. Cut out appliqué with scant 1/4" seam allowance left around the pencil line.

2. Baste under 1/4" seam allowance, making sure pencil line is hidden, clipping inside curves and corners. Pin to quilt top or secure in place with Stick 'n Stitch.

3. Set machine for blind hem stitching (3 or 4 straight stitches, then one zigzag). Set stitch length so zigzag stitches of sequence fall no farther apart than 1/4". Set stitch width so that zigzag stitch is about 1/8" wide. Thread top of machine with nylon monofilament thread, either clear or smoke color, depending on project. Thread bobbin with thread that matches the quilt top you are sewing onto. Top thread tension may need to be loosened to make sure bobbin thread does not show on the surface.

4. Sew around edges of appliqués with the straight stitches of the sequence falling on the quilt top and the zigzag stitches catching the edge of the motif. Pull top threads to back and knot with bobbin threads. Cut quilt top away from behind appliqués if you find it bulky.

Quilting:

1. Diagonal seams lines were quilted in the ditch, with lines extending through plain squares. (See quilt diagram on the previous page.)

2. Appliqués were outline quilted first and then stipple quilted.

3. The border was quilted after the quilt was bound, with lines bouncing off the inner borders and the binding. No marking is necessary since points and corners are not regular and lines do not have to be perfectly straight.

4. Add feathers or other embellishments after the quilting is done. Feathers on the bears in the sample were cut freehand from 1" x 3" scraps of Ultrasuede™. Some feathers were turned over to look like another color. The feathers were sewn to the quilt with seed beads, with the stitches kept very small on the back of the quilt and the knots hidden under the feathers.

Kokopeli
47" x 40"
Project begins
on page 45.

Double X
28" square
Project begins on page25.

Textured Pinwheels
54" x 70"
Project begins on page 67.

String Star
44" x 61"
Project begins on page 19.

Triangles Squared
54" x 66"
Project begins on page 29.

Majestic Star
48" square
Project begins
on page 15.

Snail's Trail
22" square
Project begins
on page 65.

Autumn
42" x 49"
Project begins
on page 55.

Sunflowers
30" x 37"
Project begins
on page 57.

Grid Star
42" square
Project begins on page 23.

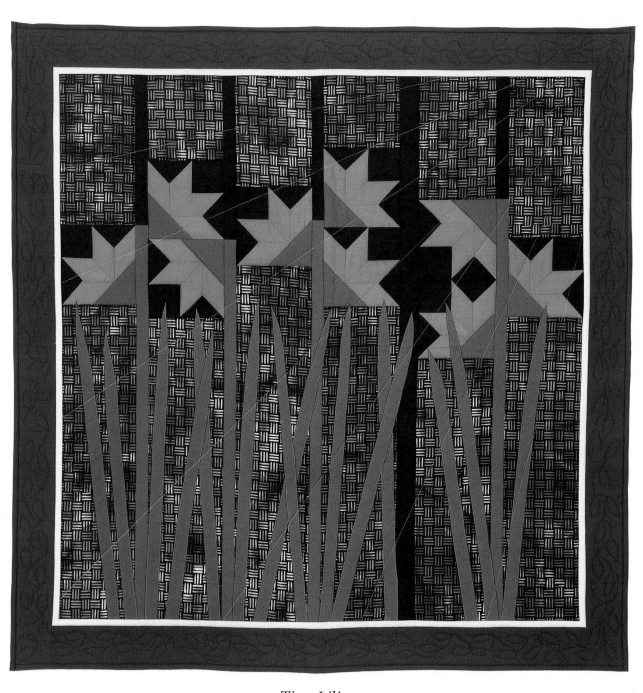

Tiger Lilies
49" square
Project begins on page 52.

Variable Star
55" square
Project begins on page 61.

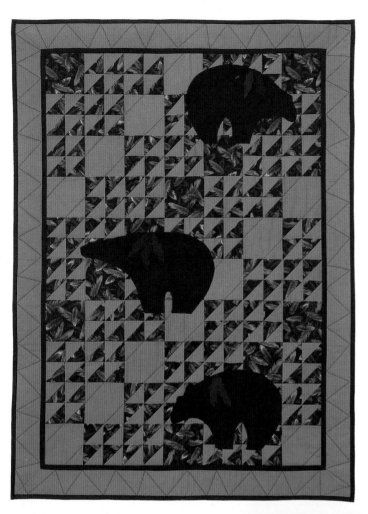

Bears
35" x 47"
Project begins on page 31.

Diamonds and Rust
40" square
Project begins on page 27.

Triangle Collage
40" x 49"
Project begins on page 70.

Hayes Corner
86" square
Project begins on page 63.

Kokopeli
47" x 40"
See Photograph page 33.

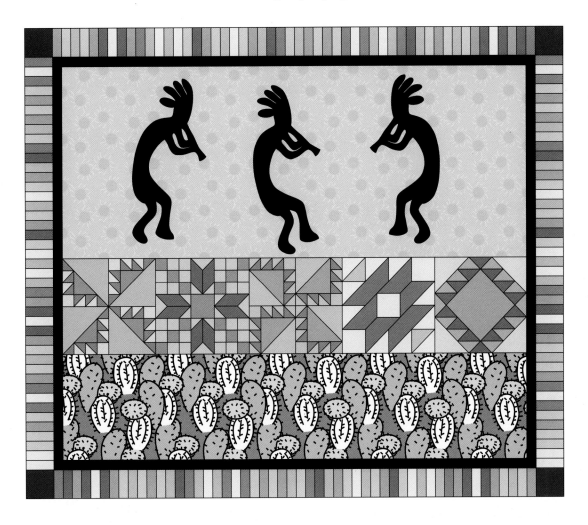

A remnant of cactus fabric was the starting point for this wallhanging which combines sampler blocks, whole cloth, and appliqué into a bold Southwestern design. The figures represent the ancient petroglyph of the Hopi Indian Kokopeli, the flute player who gives the wind its sound. The sampler blocks were chosen for their resemblance to Indian designs and the print fabric determined the color scheme. The appliqué is done with frayed edges and floats on a colorwashed printed fabric background. The bright inside border holds the different elements together and the outer border supports the pieced block section.

Materials Needed:

- one bundle of fat quarters turquoise dyed fabric
- ⅓ yard Print fabric
- small amounts of Purple fabrics for piecing, appliqué, and binding
- scrap of gray fabric for appliqué
- ½ yard bright to go with print fabric
- ½ yard Background fabric for appliqué section

Cutting Directions:

1. Cut triangles and squares for sampler blocks, referring to individual blocks below. (All block designs from *The It's Okay If You Sit On My Quilt Book* by Mary Ellen Hopkins.)

2. Cut print fabric to 9" by 40½".

3. Cut four 1" wide strips of inner border fabric.

4. Cut four 3½" squares of purple for corners of borders.

5. Cut five 2½" wide strips for binding.

6. Cut appliqués with pattern given on page 50-51. Layer three pieces of red with one piece of purple, gray, and turquoise. Cut out appliqués without seam allowances. Trim ⅛" off edges of purple, gray, and turquoise pieces.

Block Cutting/Piecing Directions:

For *Kansas Troubles* block:

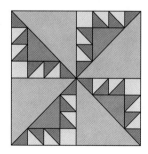

1. Cut 24 darker turquoise triangles and 16 light purple triangles from 1½" wide strips using Easy Angle™ (see page 8.)

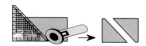

2. Cut an additional 4 squares from the light purple strip.

3. Cut two 4⅞" squares of light purple in half diagonally to make four triangles. Cut two 2⅞" squares of light turquoise in half diagonally to make four triangles.

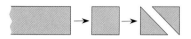

4. Piece small triangles into triangle squares.

5. Follow the graphic to piece the block. Add extra triangles and squares to form rows. Add these to the sides of the medium triangles. Piece this section to the large triangles. Sew four square units together, making sure all triangles face in the proper direction.

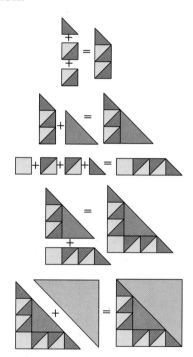

For *Stepping Stones* block:

1. Cut 12 squares of purple out of a 1½" wide strip and one more 2½" purple square.

2. Cut 24 squares of light turquoise out of a 1½" wide strip using Easy Angle™ (see page 8.)

3. Cut two 1½" wide strips of dark turquoise, then cut off end of strips at a 45°. Cut off eight 2" slices to make parallelograms.

4. Cut one 3¼" square of light turquoise with an X to make four triangles.

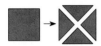

Follow the directions and graphic below for construction of the block:

1. Make four 9-patches with small turquoise and purple squares.

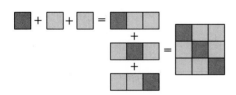

2. Sew two parallelograms together on long edges to make arrows, backstitching ¼" from end at inside corner. Sew small turquoise triangles to point of arrow. Referring to page 11 for Setting In, sew medium size turquoise triangles into inside corner, backstitching at corner. Make four of these units.

3. Sew two 9-patch blocks to one arrow block. Make two. Sew two arrow blocks to one solid square.

4. Stitch these small blocks together in a 9-patch fashion to complete the *Stepping Stones* block.

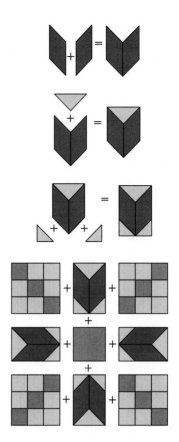

For *Navajo* block:

1. Cut 14 triangles of dark turquoise and 14 of purple out of 2" wide strips using Easy Angle™.

2. Cut two 3⅞" squares of light purple in half diagonally to make four triangles.

3. Cut one 4¾" square out of medium turquoise.

4. Sew 12 triangle squares from small turquoise and purple triangles.

5. Following the sequence below and diagram to the right, piece *Navajo* block:

Sew four sets of three triangle squares. Add small single triangles to the ends of two sets of triangle squares. Add these strips sets to the sides of the large center square. Add large purple triangles to the four corners.

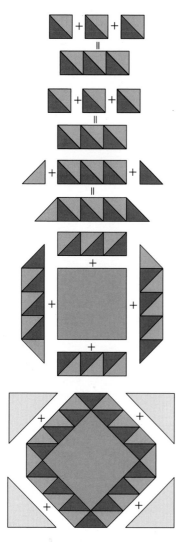

For *Rocky Mt. Puzzle* block:

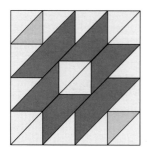

1. Cut 16 triangles of light turquoise out of a 2½" wide strip using Easy Angle™.

2. Cut a 2⅞" square of darker turquoise in half diagonally.

3. Trace trapezoid templates (found on page 50-51) onto template plastic and cut four small and two large trapezoids from the darker turquoise.

4. Follow the diagram to construct the block:

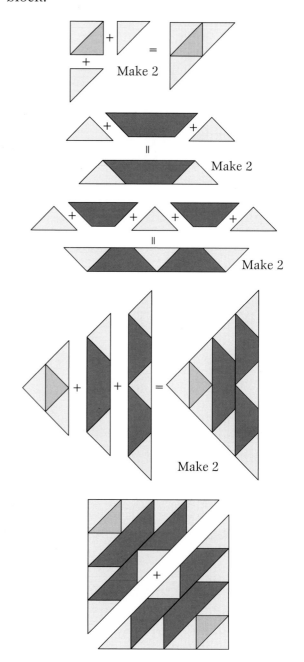

For *Indian Trails* block:

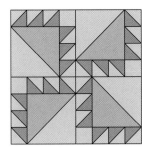

1. Cut 24 triangles of light purple and 24 triangles of turquoise out of 1½" wide strips using Easy Angle™.

2. Cut four 1½" squares of light purple.

3. Cut two 3⅞" purple squares and two of light turquoise and cut diagonally into triangles.

4. Follow the diagram below for construction of one quarter of the block. Sew 4 together for larger block.

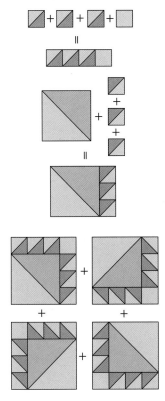

Kokopeli Appliqué:

Trace the Kokopeli appliqué on pages 50-51 onto plastic template material, lining up

the markings so that the top and bottom will be in one piece. Trace the design onto red fabric and three other colors. Place appliqués on the ½ yard of background fabric with one red figure underneath each of the other colors. Pin into place.

Topstitch ⅛" in from the edge of the top figure. Agitate this panel in the washer until the edges of the kokopeli figures fray. Trim away strings a couple of times during agitation to free up the threads. Dry in the dryer and brush the frayed edges if more fraying is desired. Press this top piece and cut to 16½" x 40½" before adding to the top of the quilt block sampler.

Piecing the Quilt Top:

1. Stitch the five blocks together in a row. Refer to the graphic on page 45, and the photograph on page 33 for larger detail.

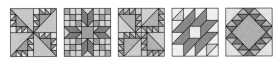

2. Add the bottom panel to the blocks.

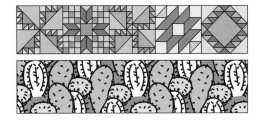

3. Add the Kokopeli panel to the blocks.

4. Measure across the middle and add inner borders. (See page 7 for details of measuring.)

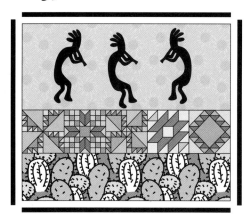

5. Cut as many 1½" strips of turquoise fabric as you have, and sew in random order side by side. Press seams to one side. Cut into 3½" wide segments. Sew end to end as shown here to make outside borders. Make two strip sets for top and bottom, and add to the quilt. Make two strip sets for sides, add purple squares to the strips then add these strips to the sides.

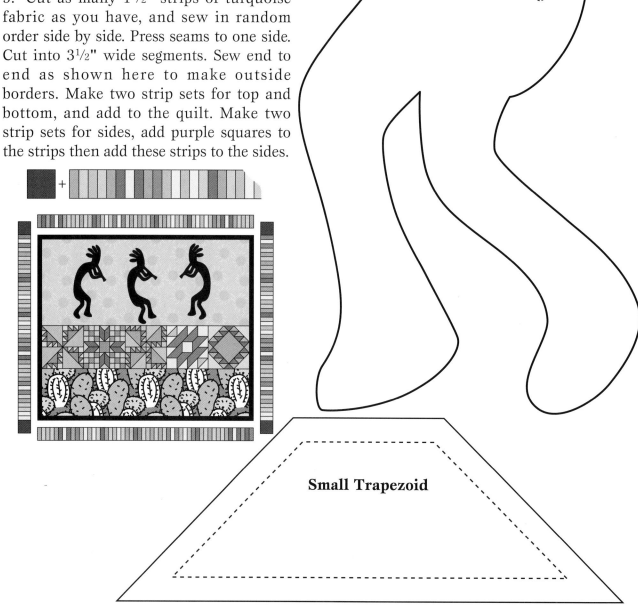

A   **A**

*Kokopeli Template
Bottom half*

Small Trapezoid

Trace both sections of the figure onto template plastic. Line up the "A" marks so that you will have one continuous figure. Cut from red – two figures facing right, and one figure facing left. Cut from three other colors, two figures facing right and one figure facing left. Trim 1/8" off edges of the three top figures so the red will show. Pin in place on top background panel. Follow directions on page 49 for complete details.

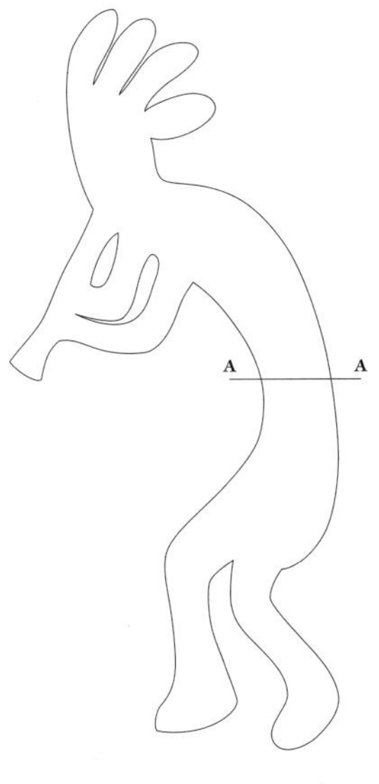

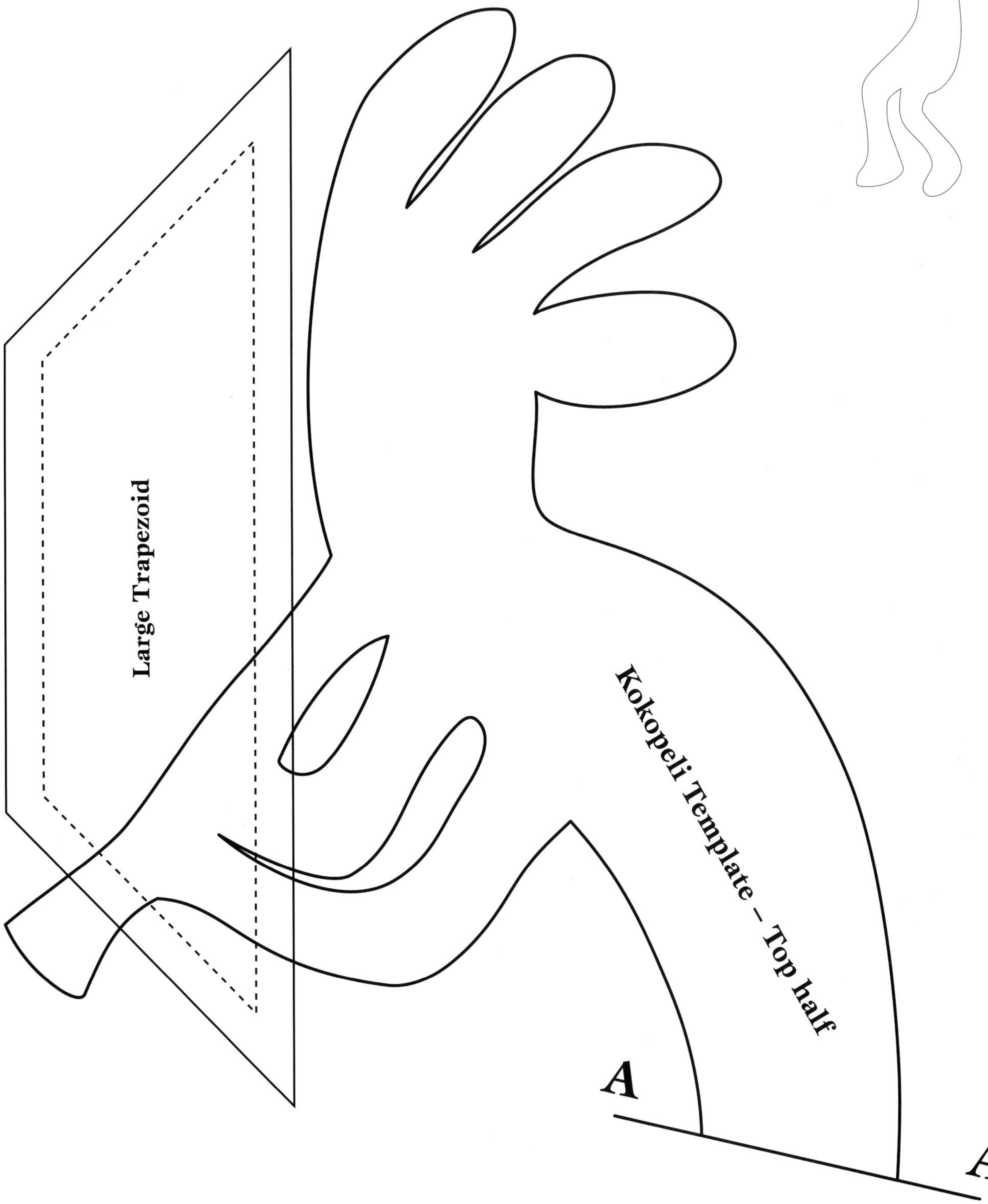

Large Trapezoid

Kokopeli Template – Top half

A

A

Tiger Lilies
49" square
See Photograph page 40.

Choose a fabric for the background of this wallhanging that says "dappled colors of a flower garden". Nine simple half stars make a cheerful array of tiger lilies and satin stitch appliqué highlights the leaves. Add a little sunshine in the color of the inner border and quilting and finish with a quilted border of vines.

Materials Needed:

- 1¹⁄₈ yard "garden" fabric for background
- ¹⁄₃ yard yard Orange for Flowers
- ⁷⁄₈ yard green for Stems, Leaves, and Bases of Flowers
- ¹⁄₃ yard Black for Background of Flower Blocks and Lattice
- ¹⁄₄ yard for Inner border
- 1 yard for Border and Binding
- Thread to match leaves

Cutting Directions:

1. Cut three 2¹⁄₄" wide strips of flower color. Following the directions on page 10, use Easy Eight™ to cut thirty-six 2¹⁄₂" diamonds.

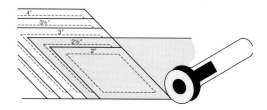

2. Cut a 4" wide strip of green into nine triangles using Easy Angle™.

3. Cut four 1¹⁄₂" wide strips of green for stems.

4. Cut fourteen 1" wide strips of green for leaves.

5. Cut two 3" wide strips of black into nine 3" squares and eighteen triangles.

6. Cut two 1¹⁄₂" wide strips and one 2" wide strip of black.

7. Cut garden fabric lengthwise into six 6¹⁄₂" wide by 1¹⁄₈ yard strips.

8. Cut four or five (depending on fabric width) 1" wide strips for inner border.

9. Cut five 3¹⁄₂" wide strips for outer border.

10. Cut five 2¹⁄₂" wide strips for binding.

Piecing Directions:

1. Piece pairs of diamonds together, backstitching at wide angle.

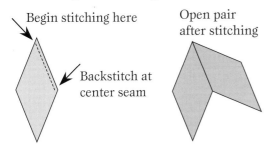

Begin stitching here

Open pair after stitching

Backstitch at center seam

2. Piece two pairs in same manner to make half of an eight-point star flower.

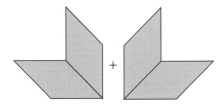

3. Follow the directions on page 11 for setting in the triangles and squares.

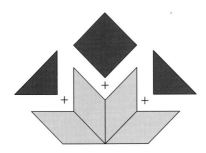

4. Fold green triangle in half, finger crease. Match crease to center of flower and stitch across for base. Press seams away from flower. Make 9 flowers.

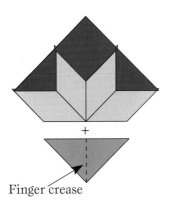

Finger crease

5. The six background strips you have cut, will be cut again into two sections. The flower blocks will be sewn between the two sections of each. Cut sections as follows: 1st row, cut 12" from top; 2nd row, cut 7" from top; 3rd row, cut 9"; 4th row cut 6"; 5th row, cut 10"; 6th row cut 13" from the top.

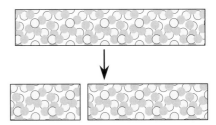

Add one or two blocks between cut edges as in photo. Excess fabric at bottom of the rows will be trimmed off later.

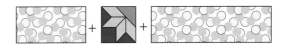

6. Cut 1½" black strips in half and piece end to end to green stem strips. Position seam intersections where it appears most natural. Sew strips between the rows of flowers. Sew the 2" black strip between fourth and fifth row where there are no flower base connections. Trim off excess at top. Press seams toward stems.

53

7. Fold quilt top in half vertically, check to see if top edge is straight and trim, if not. Trim off excess fabric at the bottom of the quilt, so length measures the same as width (approximately 42").

8. Cut the 1" wide green strips into 20"-24" lengths with tapering at the ends for leaves. (Cut by hand for slight differences in width and tips.) Line up leaves with bottom edge of quilt top, and randomly angle toward flowers. Secure in place with Stitck 'n Stitch.

9. After all stems are positioned and anchored to the quilt top, you are ready to machine appliqué. (Again I reference *Mastering Machine Appliqué*, by Harriett Hargrave for this technique.) Set machine for a $1/8$" wide satin stitch and short stitch length that covers the edge of leaves. Sew from bottom of leaves, tapering stitch at tips of leaves by narrowing the stitch width, pivot and sew back to bottom. Use a strip of newsprint paper under quilt top as you sew each leaf to stabilize the fabric and prevent puckering. Press.

10. Following the directions on page 7 for determining length to cut your borders, cut and sew the inner and outer borders to quilt top. Sew the side borders first, then the top and bottom.

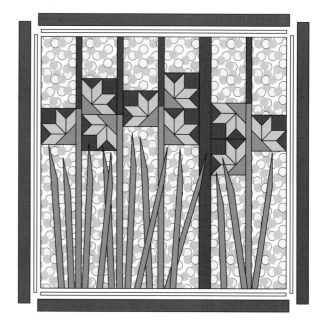

11. After ditch quilting seam lines of leaves and flowers, draw sun ray lines in chalk across quilt, lining up one end of yardstick with outer corner of quilt and fanning out over flowers. Quilt with gold metallic thread, using a #14 needle instead of the usual #12. The seam between the inner and outer borders can also be quilted with gold thread. Use a darning foot and no feed dogs to free motion quilt a vine on the outer border.

Autumn
42" x 49"
See Photograph page 38.

Materials Needed:

- 1 yard sky fabric
- scraps of "rock" fabric
- $3/4$ yard brown solid for branch
- 2 dozen polyester leaves
- nylon filament thread
- $7/8$ yard for border and binding

Cutting Directions:

1. Straighten edges of the sky fabric with the Quickline Ruler and rotary cutter.

2. Following the directions on pages 12-13, cut 32 hexagons from $4^{7}/8$" strips using the Easy Hexagon™ tool.

3. Cut the tree branch using the pattern on the insert at the back of the book. Do not add seam allowances.

4. Cut five $3^{1}/2$" strips of border fabric. Cut five $2^{1}/2$" wide strips for binding.

Piecing Directions:

1. Hang the sky fabric on a design wall and arrange the hexagons on it using the diagram below and the photo on page 38 as guides. Pin hexagons in place so that you can carry the project to the sewing machine. (Hexagons will be sewn separately and applied to the background later.)

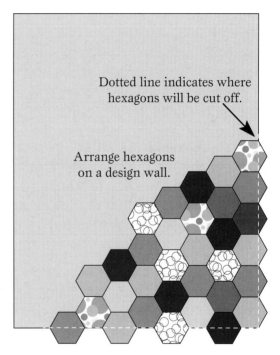

Dotted line indicates where hexagons will be cut off.

Arrange hexagons on a design wall.

2. Sew hexagons together. Mark intersections of seam allowances and sew between marks, backstitching at each intersection.

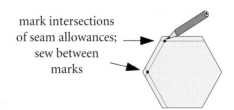

mark intersections of seam allowances; sew between marks

3. Press hexagons and trim off the right side and bottom edges to be straight. Turn under ¼" seam allowances on upper edges and pin to sky fabric.

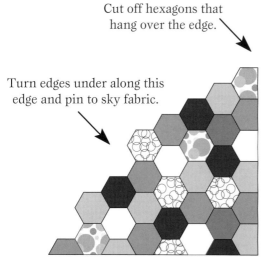

Cut off hexagons that hang over the edge.

Turn edges under along this edge and pin to sky fabric.

4. Use blind hem stitch appliqué and nylon monofilament thread to appliqué the upper edges to the sky fabric. (Refer to *Bears* design pages 31-32. A good source book is *Mastering Machine Appliqué*, by Harriett Hargrave.) Hint: If nylon thread breaks, place spool on floor in a jar or basket so it can unwind freely. In the sample on page 38 you will notice I have placed two small branches on this hexagon rock hill. This is a design option and no template is given.

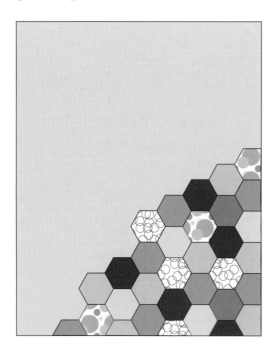

5. Glue-stick branch to background and satin stitch edges. Add borders, baste, quilt and bind. Quilting is done in the ditch of the hexagon seams and swirls are quilted in the sky to indicate a breeze.

6. After quilt is finished, add pre-purchased leaves. Peal plastic stems from back of leaves. Pin leaves to quilt as if swirling in the air. Using nylon filament thread, quilt veins into leaves all the way to the tips to hold them in place.

Sunflowers
30" x 37"
See Photograph page 38.

Make a sunny wallhanging for a kitchen or child's room using the Easy Hexagon™ to cut the honeycomb background. Dresden Plate sunflowers are fun to make and leaves and flower points are three dimensional for a lively look.

Materials Needed:

- ¼ yards of eight background fabrics OR 1 bundle of eight fat quarters of dyed fabrics
- 1 yard for border and binding
- ½ yard sunflower fabric
- scraps of brown print for flower centers
- ¼ yard leaf fabric

Cutting Directions:

1. Cut one 5¾" wide strip of each of the eight background fabrics. Following the directions on page 12-13, and using the largest size (3") on the tool, cut 30 hexagons.

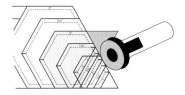

2. Cut four 4½" and four 2½" wide strips of border fabric.

3. Cut three 4¼" wide strips of flower fabric. Trace template for petal onto plastic and cut 48 petals from these strips.

4. Trace template for leaves onto plastic and cut ten leaves.

Piecing Directions:

1. Arrange 30 hexagons on a design wall to balance colors, as in the diagram and photo on page 38. Work in vertical rows. Sew hexagons together, one seam at a time, as indicated in diagram below.

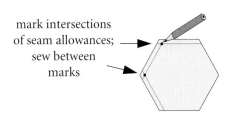

mark intersections of seam allowances; sew between marks

2. With rotary cutter and Quikline Ruler, cut off the top and bottom edges of the quilt top even with the edges of the inner hexagon edges. Cut off sides along innermost raw edges.

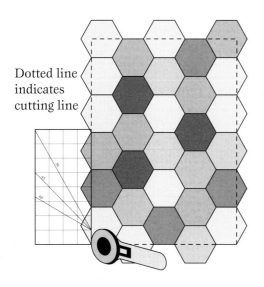

Dotted line indicates cutting line

3. Add top and bottom borders, then add side borders.

4. Fold petals in half lengthwise, right sides together, and sew across wide ends with $1/4$" seam allowance. Turn points right side out and press with seams down the center back of the petal.

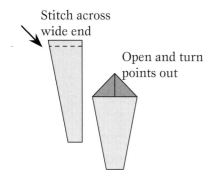

Stitch across wide end

Open and turn points out

5. Sew 16 petals together into circle, backstitching at folded edges. Press seams in one direction. Make three flowers.

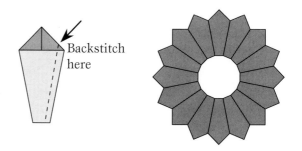

Backstitch here

6. Cut circle template from template plastic. Cut three flower centers from brown print fabric. Secure seam allowances to the back of the fabric using Stitck 'n Stitch. Position circles on flowers using Stitck 'n Stitch to hold. Blind hem stitch in place. (See *Bears*, page 32.)

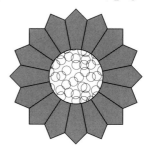

7. Place two leaf pieces right sides together and sew around entire outside edge with $1/4$" seam allowance. Cut a small slit in the back of one layer of the leaf and pull leaf right side out. Press.

Stich 2 leaves together

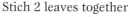
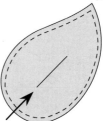

Cut a slit in one leaf.
Pull right sides of leaves out through the slit.

8. Position flowers and leaves on the quilt top and hold in place with Stitck 'n Stitch.

9. Quilt around flowers at base of tips so the tips remain free, but catching leaves. Quilt around flower centers and in seams of visible hexagons. Quilt veins into leaves to hold them in place.

10. In the sample shown on page 38, I did not quilt in the borders. However, Stitch-Thru™ #6105, Fleur is the perfect size for these borders. The completed quilt graphic show this design in the borders.

11. Bind with 2½" strips.

When you quilt across the tip of the flower, you will anchor the leaf in place.

SUNFLOWER
PETAL
TEMPLATE

DO NOT ADD
SEAM
ALLOWANCE

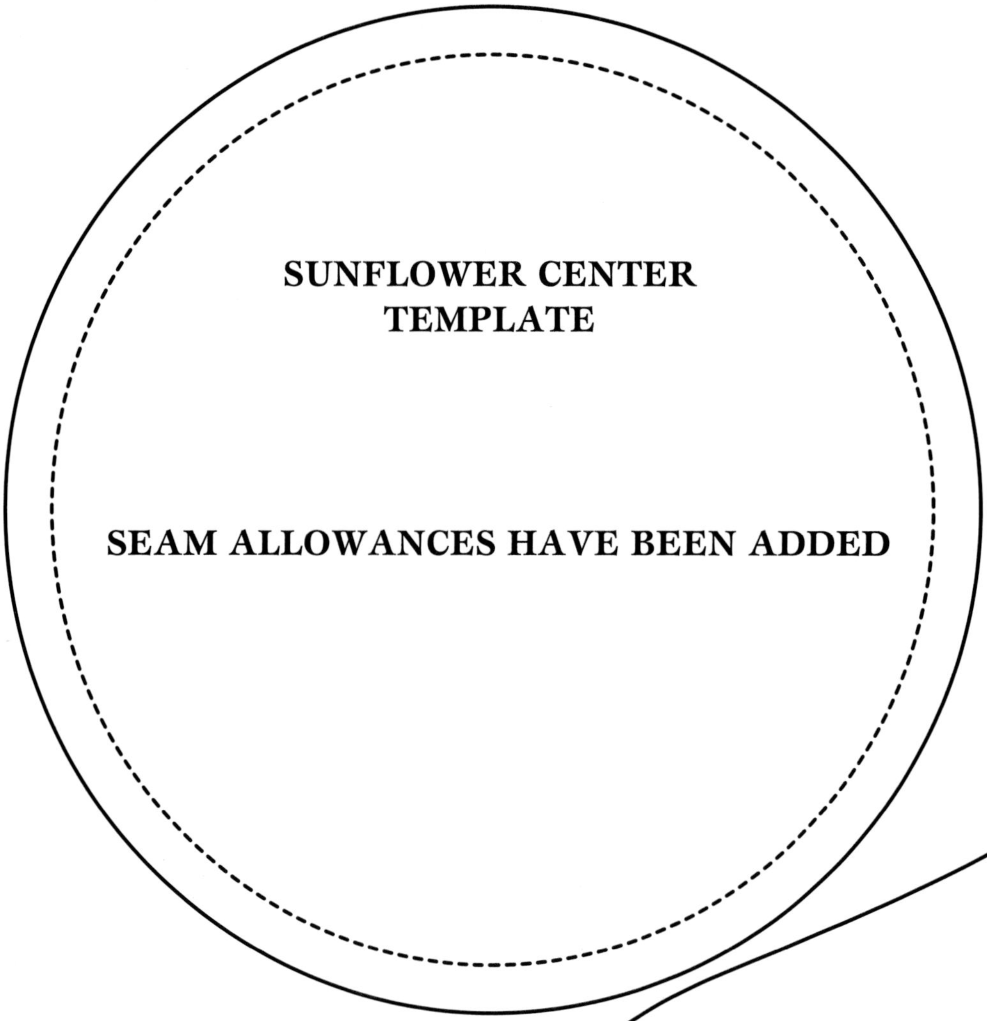

**SUNFLOWER CENTER
TEMPLATE**

SEAM ALLOWANCES HAVE BEEN ADDED

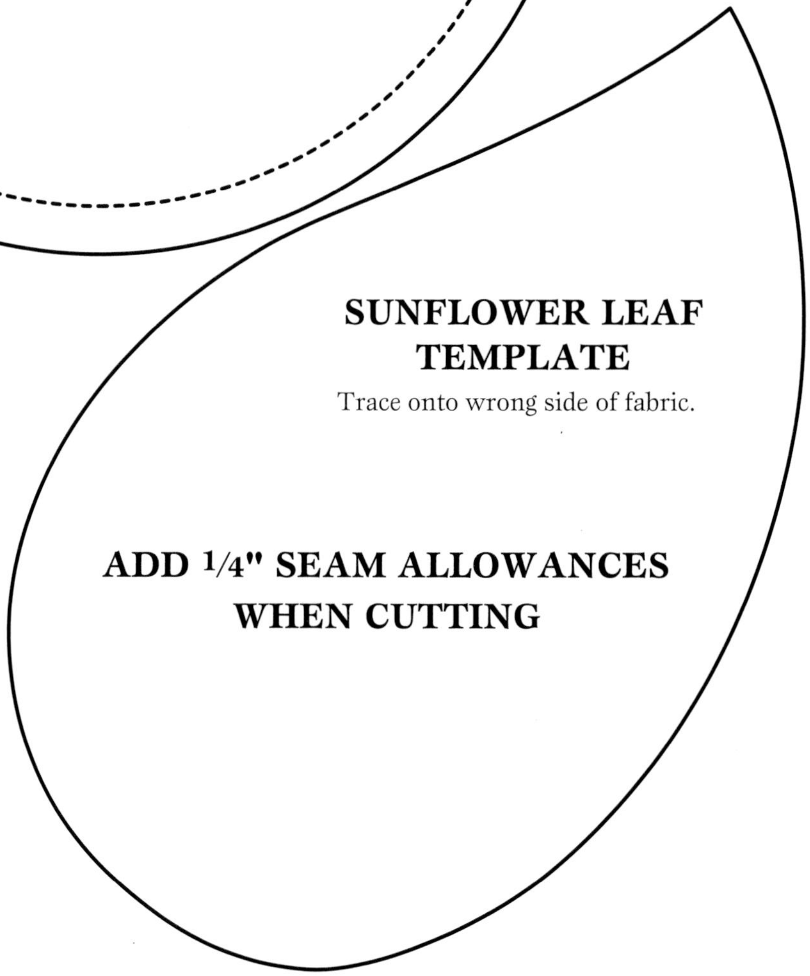

**SUNFLOWER LEAF
TEMPLATE**

Trace onto wrong side of fabric.

**ADD 1/4" SEAM ALLOWANCES
WHEN CUTTING**

Variable Star

55" square
See Photograph page 41.

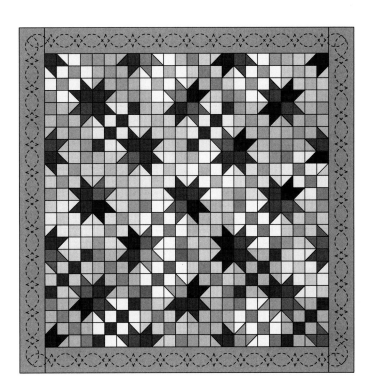

This quilt is made up of scraps of turquoise, rust, peach, and purple solids. Again, a reason to collect every solid you see. Since the block is 8" square, it is easy to adapt the size of the quilt to any use you wish, from the lap robe size of the sample to king size. The quilt is also very attractive done in prints as long as you remember to keep enough contrast between the colors so the chains and stars stand out. Do as many blocks as you like and then arrange them on the wall until you get the effect you want – don't try to coordinate everything ahead of time.

Materials Needed:

- ¼ yards or scraps of turquoise, rust, peach, and purple solids
- 1 yard for Borders
- ⅝ yard for Binding

Cutting Directions:

1. Cut 216 -2½" squares of peach background.

2. For each block: cut two 2½" squares and four 2½" triangles of rust using Easy Angle™ (see page 8).

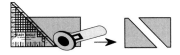

3. For each block: cut four 2½" squares of either purple or turquoise.

4. Cut eight 4" wide strips of border fabric.

5. Cut six 2½" wide strips of binding fabric.

Piecing Directions:

1. For each block: Sew four background triangles to four rust triangles to make triangle squares. Cut off points.

2. Sew squares and traingle squares together referring to the photo on page 41, using purple squares in half of the blocks, and turquoise in the other half. The purple and turquoise blocks will form the diagonal chains. The black/white diagram may not be as accurate in value placement as the photograph. Make 36 blocks. Press blocks.

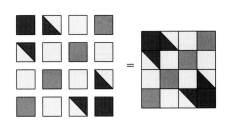

61

3. Arrange blocks so purple chain goes in one direction through quilt top and turquoise chain goes in the opposite direction. Sew into rows and attach rows together.

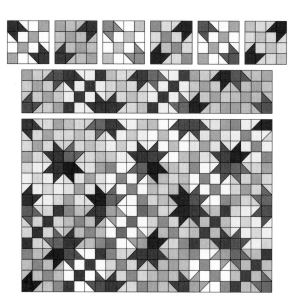

4. Piece borders and add to top and bottom edges, then sides.

5. In the sample in the photo on page 41, the quilting is done in the ditch of the blocks and channel quilting is used in the borders. In the example below, Stitch-Thru™ #6101, Peaks and Valleys is used.

Hayes Corner
86" square
See Photograph page 44.

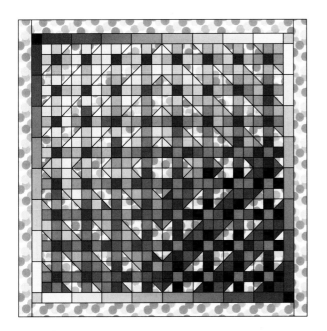

Hayes Corner is a popular Amish quilt pattern and is often copied in a traditional color scheme. Here a batik fabric combines with two dyed gradations and a solid magenta for an exciting contemporary look. This size is perfect for a queen sized coverlet, to be used with pillow shams. It is also easy to adapt to any other size bed or wall – just get out graph paper and redraw the simple diagram to your specifications.

Materials Needed:

- one bundle of ½ yards of dyed fabric in purple gradation
- one bundle of ½ yards of dyed fabric in navy gradation
- ¾ yard magenta fabric for connecting squares
- 2⅝ yards print fabric with non-directional pattern.

Cutting Directions:

1. From each of the eight purple values cut thirty-two 3½" squares. Cut 4 extra squares for the inner border corner pieces.

2. From connecting square fabric cut sixty-four 3½" squares.

3. From each of the eight navy values cut eight 3½" squares and sixteen 3½" triangles using Easy Angle™. (See page 8.)

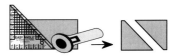

4. Cut one 3½" wide strip of each navy value into four 9½" rectangles.

5. From print fabric cut four 4½" wide by 2⅝ yard long borders from lengthwise grain. From fabric remaining cut 3½" wide strips into sixty-four 3½" squares and 128 triangles using Easy Angle™. (See page 8.)

6. Cut ten 2½" wide strips from darker navy fabrics for binding.

Piecing Directions:

1. Arrange squares and triangles on a design wall, with dark values of purple and navy at one corner, working into light values at opposite corner. Try to have only a few places where the same color is touching itself.

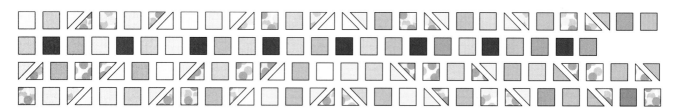

2. After laying each piece for the quilt on a design wall, carry one row at a time to the sewing machine. The first four rows are shown above. Notice the triangles are treated as individual blocks in the row at this point. Stitch the triangles together first to make triangle squares, then replace them in the row. Stitch each block together to form the finished row. Continue stitching each row until all rows are finished, then stitch the rows together.

3. Connect navy rectangles end to end in order of value – dark to light. See full graphic below and refer to the photograph on page 44. On two of these border strips add the 3½" purple squares to the ends. Sew borders to the quilt top matching appropriate seam lines.

4. Follow directions for borders on page 7 for measuring and cutting borders. Sew outer borders to the quilt top. Press.Bind with 2½" strips. Ditch quilt in all vetical and horizontal seams.

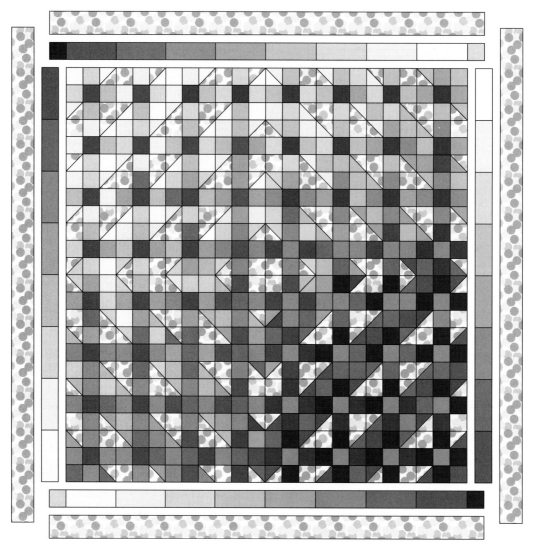

Snail's Trail
22" square
See Photograph page 37.

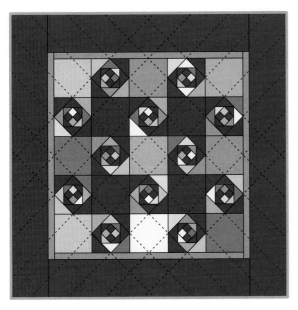

Snail's Trail or Monkey Wrench is a fun pattern to play with and makes a great gift in this small size. For bed quilts or a larger wallhanging simply increase the block size by drawing a larger square on paper and dividing the sides in half to get the next inside square and continuing toward the center until the block is all drawn. Measure the new pieces you have drawn and add ¼" seam allowances on all edges for the new sizes you will need. Quilting on the sample is simply done in an overall grid of diamonds sewn in metallic thread.

Materials Needed:

- one bundle of eight fat eighths, multiple colors (from Shades)
- ½ yard Gray solid for alternate blocks and outer borders.
- ⅛ yard for Inner border
- ¼ yard for Binding

Cutting Directions:

1. From the bundle of fat eighths cut a total of 24 triangles from 2" wide strips using Easy Angle™. See page 8 for complete instructions.

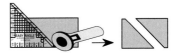

2. From the fat eighths cut a total of 24 triangles from 1½" wide strips using Easy Angle™. See page 8 for details.

3. From the fat eighths cut a total of 24 triangles from 1¼" wide strips with Easy Angle™. See page 8 for details.

4. Cut 24 triangles of each size (2", 1½", 1¼") from the gray solid using Easy Angle™. See page 8 for details.

5. Cut 24 -1" squares from the fat eighths colors and 24 -1" squares from the gray.

6. Cut nine 3½" squares from fat eighths colors and four 3½" squares from gray.

7. Cut two inner borders 1" x 15½" and two 1" x 16½".

8. Cut two outer borders 3½" x 16½" and two 3½" x 22½".

9. Cut 2" wide strips for binding.

Piecing Directions:

1. Piece two colored and two gray 1" squares into a four-patch for the center of each block.

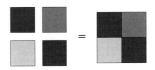

65

2. Add two colored and two gray small triangles to each four patch as in diagram, lining up center point of triangles with seams of four patch. Press seams away from center.

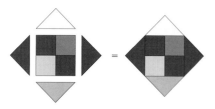

3. Add medium triangles and then larger triangles in same manner to complete blocks. Make 12 blocks. Press.

4. Arrange blocks with plain squares as in photo, making sure overall design is as planned. Stitch blocks together into rows, then sew the rows together.

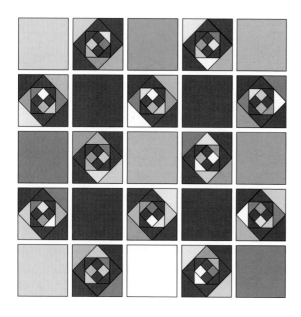

5. Add inner and outer borders. Refer to the measuring and cutting instructions on page 7 for more details.

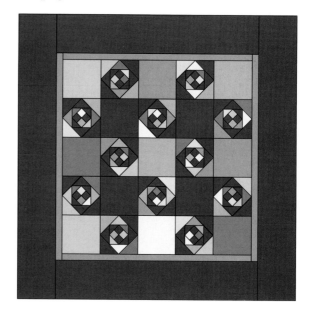

6. Mark diagonal lines across quilt with a chalk wheel. Extend the lines through the plain blocks and borders.

7. Quilt and bind with 2" strips.

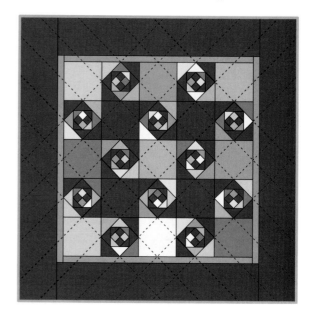

66

Textured Pinwheels

54" x 70"
See Photograph page 34.

If you use fabric that is the same on both sides (like the hand dyed "snakeskin" in the sample) for the pinwheels it will be a snap to make this textured twin sized quilt because it will require no special thought to piece and the blocks are very simple. The texture comes from using the blocks on the wrong side – the seam allowances fray and create the texture.

Materials Needed:

- one bundle of six fat quarters of dyed fabric (color: "Overdye-snakeskin cherry red" – Lunn Fabrics)
- 1 yard for background fabric
- 2¼ yards fabric for lattice and borders
- ⅔ yard binding fabric

Cutting Directions:

1. Cut each of the six dyed fat quarters into four $3\frac{1}{2}$" wide strips and one $2\frac{1}{2}$" wide strip. Cut the $3\frac{1}{2}$" wide strips into triangles using Easy Angle™. Cut the $2\frac{1}{2}$" wide strips into squares for lattice.

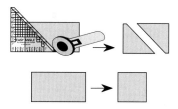

2. Cut background fabric into $3\frac{1}{2}$" wide strips and then cut into 192 triangles using Easy Angle™.

3. Cut four strips of border fabric $4\frac{1}{2}$" wide by $2\frac{1}{4}$ yards from lengthwise grain. Cut eighty-two $2\frac{1}{2}$" x $6\frac{1}{2}$" rectangles from remaining fabric for lattice.

4. Cut seven $2\frac{1}{2}$" wide strips of binding fabric.

Piecing Directions:

1. Sew colored triangles to background triangles to make triangle squares.

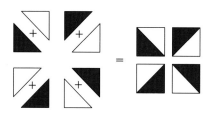

Take into consideration when piecing that the sewing thread will show. The wrong side becomes the right side of the quilt! If you choose a print fabric instead of the hand-dyed, you may not want to texture this project.

2. Press seam allowances toward background. Sew two triangles squares together, then sew these pairs of triangles squares together butting seams at the center of the block. Make a total of 48 blocks. Press and trim off points.

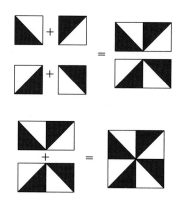

3. Arrange blocks into eight rows of six blocks each. Refer to the photograph on page 34 and the full graphic on page 67. The "wrong" side – the side with the seams showing is now the "right" side of the block. Connect the blocks (seams of blocks are showing on the top) with lattice strips between each block. Press seams toward lattice.

4. Make seven lattice strip rows of six rectangles and five connecting squares.

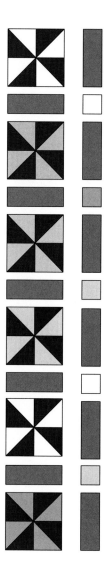

68

5. Connect rows of blocks – wrong side of blocks – to right sides of lattice strips.

6. Follow directions on page 7 for measuring and sewing border strips. The borders for this quilt were cut from the lengthwise grain of the fabric. Add borders to the top and bottom of the quilt, then add the borders to sides. When pressing quilt top at this point do not worry about "messing up" the exposed seams on fronts of the blocks.

7. Choose a batt that needs to be quilted only every 6" and will withstand machine washing. Baste layers and quilt along lattice. Bind edges with 2½" wide strips.

8. Machine wash quilt with no soap, clipping threads that loosen from edges to promote fraying. Dry by machine until only slightly damp. Shake out wrinkles and clip threads again. Finish drying flat or over two clotheslines. Brush seams if more fraying is desired.

9. Ditch quilting was done in all the horizontal and verical seams, extending all the way through the borders. If you prefer, you may want to use one of the Stitch-Thru™ cable designs or another border design.

Triangle Collage

40" x 49"
See Photograph page 43.

This is a just-for-fun wallhanging where you can use leftover pieces of other projects, plus buttons, beads, and ribbons. Use the sample for a jumping off place and see where your imagination leads you.

Materials Needed:

- Scraps of dyed fabrics
- 1 yard background fabric with woven grid or plaid.
- 1¼ yard grosgrain ribbon (³⁄₈" wide)
- Beads, buttons, nylon monofilament thread
- 1 yard Border and Binding fabric.

Cutting Directions:

1. Cut leftover pieces of dyed fabric into various sizes of triangles using Easy Angle™.

2. Cut and straighten edges of background fabric to 33½" x 42½", following grid or plaid in fabric.

3. Cut five 4" wide strips for borders and five 2½" wide strips for binding.

Piecing Directions:

1. Secure ribbon to the background fabric with Stitck 'n Stitch. Sew with invisible thread along one edge.

2. Pin this piece of background fabric to a design wall. Arrange various size triangles along woven lines in the fabric and pin in place, tucking blunt points of triangles under unsewn edge of ribbon and each other. Avoid using too many triangles – leave some "breathing space" for the eye to rest on. Refer to the photograph on page 43 and the layout to the right for ideas. Use your imagination to create your own personal collage. After you are satisfied with the layout, secure pieces in place with Stitck 'n Stitch.

3. Sew around the edges of triangles with invisible thread ⅛" from raw edges

4. Sew along remaining edge of ribbon. Press quilt top from wrong side.

5. Follow directions on page 7 for measuring and cutting for borders. Add borders to the top and bottom, then to the sides of the quilt.

6. Quilt along lines in plaid or grid of fabric, extending lines across borders, or quilt triangles of various sizes into borders.

7. Sew beads and buttons to quilt, sliding the needle between the layers of the quilt to get from one location to another and hiding the knots in the batting as in hand quilting. Bind quilt.

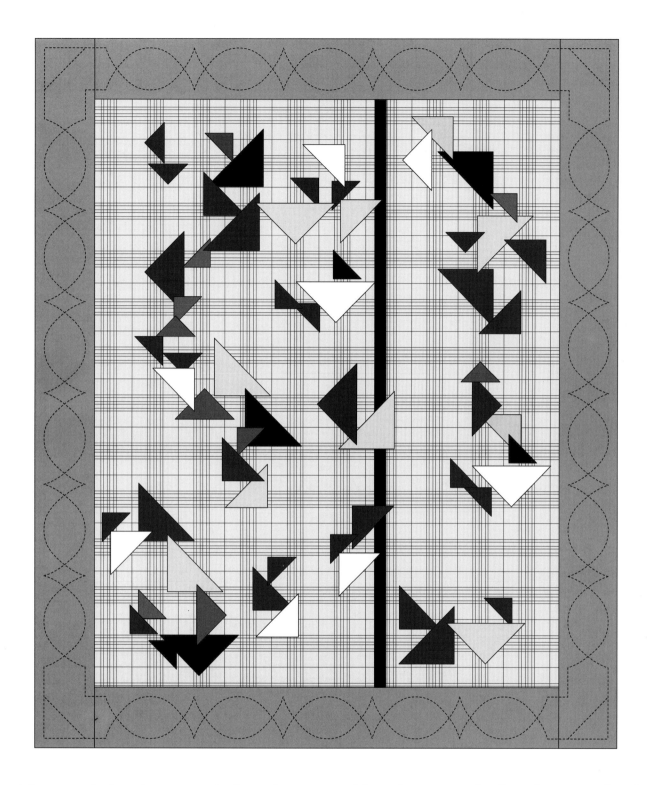

After completing the top, again hang it on a design wall and add embellishments such as beads, buttons, ribbon, whatever you feel will enhance the collage look. Make it your own personal design.

Many items can be found at your local craft or fabric store. Look in your sewing kits and you may find some old buttons or pieces of ribbon left from other projects.

About the Author

Susan began making quilts in 1977 and since that time has made hundreds of quilts, wallhangings, liturgical hangings, and quilted garments. A very busy woman – she has owned a quilt shop, worked in two others, been state guild president, a national quilt show chairman, and taught many classes.

Susan has consulted on the two Singer Reference Library quilting books and contributed to several other Singer books. Her quilts have been published in various books and magazines and exhibited in numerous locations. Her special interests are samplers with innovative settings, the use of dyed fabrics, and Double Wedding Ring quilts with contemporary effects created with texture and appliqué. She loves to design new looks for old patterns and share her ideas with others and feels quilting opens up many opportunities for women to express themselves and discover talents for the first time.

Susan lives in St. Paul, Minnesota, in a restored Victorian house with her husband and 100 quilts. She has two grown children who decorate their homes with her work.

Bibliography

Hargrave, Harriet, *Mastering Machine Appliqué*. Lafayette, Ca.: C & T Publishing, 1991.

Hopkins, Mary Ellen, *The It's Okay If You Sit On My Quilt Book*. Santa Monica, Ca.: ME Publications, 1989.

Other Fine Quilting Books From EZ International

Traditional Quilts, The Easy Way, Sharon Hultgren
Traditional Quilts II, Sharon Hultgren
Companions, Quilts & Miniatures, Darlene Zimmerman
Winning Ways, Connie Hester
Picking Up the Pieces, Piecemakers